The House That Jack Built

Also by James Haskins

AMISTAD PRESS

AN IMPRINT OF HARPERCOLLINS*PUBLISHERS*

The House That Jack Built

MY LIFE STORY AS A TRAILBLAZER IN BROADCASTING AND ENTERTAINMENT

with James Haskins

HarperCollins books may be purchased for educational, business, or sales promotional use. For information, please write: Special Markets Department, HarperCollins Publishers Inc., 10 East 53rd Street, New York NY 10022.

FIRST EDITION

Book design by Claire Naylon Vaccaro

Library of Congress Cataloging-in-Publication Data
Jackson, Hal.
The house that Jack built: my life story as a trailblazer in broadcasting and entertainment/Hal Jackson with James Haskins.
p.   cm.
ISBN 0-06-019847-8
1. Jackson, Hal. 2. Radio broadcasters—United States—Biography.
3. African American radio broadcasters—United States—Biography.
I. Haskins, James, 1941–   . II. Title.
PN1991.4.J33 A3 2001
791.44'028'092—dc21
[B]   00-046900

01 02 03 04 ❖/RRD 10 9 8 7 6 5 4 3 2 1

To my wife Debi
and all of our Talented Teen International contestants

every **SATURDAY** & **SUNDAY** Afternoon

the ampeg sound

PRESENTS

TOP RECORDING STARS
IN PERSON

record world  SHOW

PRODUCED BY

RADIO & TV PERSONALITY

HAL
JACKSON

AT

PALISADES AMUSEMENT PARK N.J.

HALF MILE SOUTH OF GEO. WASHINGTON BRIDGE

250 **SATURDAYS 3-5 P.M.**

HAL BROADCASTS LIVE DIRECT

ACKNOWLEDGMENTS

Thank you Charles Harris. You are the captain that finally gave wings to a project that seemed to have gone on forever.

Jim Haskins took my feelings and life in through his ears and wrote what I felt in my heart. Thank you for the many hours we spent together.

Mel Watkins came to the rescue when we thought all was lost. Thanks for being there.

Kajuana Haulsey made me see the colorful flowers that grew in the garden of my life. You are truly a treasure in the literary world.

A large thank you to all of you who have been a part of my life and therefore a part of the person I am today. You are loved. Remember, it's nice to be important, but it's more important to be nice.

INTRODUCTION

The Washington, D.C., I came to in 1935 was a quiet, beautiful city. It was not only the capital of the United States, but also the totally segregated capital of Jim Crow.

My father was the Turkish ambassador to the United States and my brother Nesuhi and I were avid jazz fans. We had Sunday lunches and fun sessions at the embassy for local musicians and members of touring orchestras, such as Duke Ellington, Benny Carter, Tommy Dorsey, and Count Basie, pianists Meade Lux Lewis and Peter Johnson, and blues singer Big Joe Turner. Some Southern senators objected to all this, but my father supported us.

Nesuhi and I made friends with some outstanding members of the Black community: physician Dr. Thomas Williston, the dean of the Howard University Department of English Literature, author Sterling Brown, architect Granville Hurley, psychology professor Eugene Holmes, actor Canada Lee, young pianist Billy Taylor, Judge William Hastie, among many others.

We also organized Washington's first integrated concerts. We produced jazz concerts with Black and White performers onstage and a Black and White audience for the first time.

But then I also made friends with people I met backstage at the Howard Theater, and at the many nightclubs and after-hours places that flourished in those years. They included "My Man Harvey," a big numbers operator; blues singer Rubberlegs Williams; and Cab Calloway's sister Blanche Calloway, who was the manager of the Crystal Caverns, a basement nightclub featuring drummer Streamline Burrell and other members of the Black D.C. demimonde.

All those people shared one thing: They were not accepted in the Whites-only establishments, including department stores, theaters, movie houses, restaurants, hotels, and rest-rooms. It is difficult today to realize how oppressive it was so recently.

During the years of the Second World War, things began to loosen up a bit. While I was going to graduate school at Georgetown University, I began to think earnestly about start-ing a record company. After two false starts, including an at-tempted partnership with Lionel Hampton (Atlantic might have been called Hampt-Tone Records), I borrowed $10,000 from my dentist, and with Herb and Miriam Abramson as my partners, I started Atlantic Records in 1947.

It was in this atmosphere that I first met Harold Jackson.

We started to release our first records in 1948, but getting played on radio was another matter. I had been going around to radio stations with not too much success. One of the people who was nice to me from the beginning was Hal Jackson. He had a show on WUST, which had studios on U Street NW in Washington's Black ghetto.

Hal was a natural winner. He was young and good-looking, with a wonderful bubbly personality. He had no complexes and treated everyone the same way, whether it was the owner of the station or the waiter in a restaurant, and whether he was addressing Black or White. He lived as if segregation did not exist, although he suffered immensely through it.

Hal was always cheerful, but in a real way, not put on. Most of all, not only was he very cordial toward me, but he helped me in my greatest hour of need. He broke my first records in Washington.

One sure way to get radio play was to make a record a disk jockey would agree to use as a theme song. So I wrote and recorded an instrument we called *The Blues That Jack Built*, after Hal's show *The House That Jack Built*. It featured a young Washington saxophonist named Billy Williams, and thanks to Harold, it became something of a hit. I scatted a riff along with my friend Julio Mario Santo Domingo, who is now chairman of the giant brewery Bavaria, and Avianca, the Colombian airline.

The next time I saw Harold was at Turner's Arena, Washington's Madison Square Garden, where his professional basketball team, coached by Red Auerbach, was playing a game. That's the first time I sat on a bench at a pro game. I couldn't believe that our Harold Jackson was the organizer of this great team.

But Harold was a keen entrepreneur who loved what he was doing. He dearly loved sports, music, and broadcasting, and it was not surprising that he became so successful in his career.

I am proud to have been Hal Jackson's friend for so many years, and I want to take this opportunity to thank him once more for all the help he gave me when I started the smallest company in the United States. And since (smile).

Love you, Harold,

Ahmet Ertegun

The House That Jack Built

AIR CONDITIONED
Showplace of Harlem

APOLLO

125th ST. near 8th AVE.

LA WEEK BEG. **FRI. JULY 8**

STATION WLIB's POPULAR **HAL JACKSON**

RHYTHM AND **BLUES SHOW**

ARNETT COBB AND BAND

WILLIE MABON · THE CADILLACS

ANNIE LAURIE · **WALKIN' WILLIE** · JIMMIE SCOTT

HONEYTONES · **BOP & LOCK** · TITUS TURNER

Wed. Nite: AMATEURS | Sat. MIDNITE SHOW

1190 ON THE DIAL

WLIB

HARLEM RADIO CENTER   2090 Seventh Avenue · Hot

I.

CHARLESTON TO WASHINGTON

s was the case with many Blacks of my generation born in the South, my birth was not officially recorded. I was born at home, not in a hospital, and the church my family attended did not keep birth records in any organized fashion. This circumstance later caused me considerable frustration when I tried to get a passport and other official documents requiring proof of birth. But as narrowly as I can pinpoint it, I was born on November 3, 1915, in Charleston, South Carolina. I was the fifth child, and third son, of Eugene Baron Jackson and Laura Rivers Jackson. My given name was Harold Baron Jackson, but I was never called Harold. My childhood nickname was Peaches, or Peachy, because when I was a baby I didn't like peaches. Later on, when I decided that nickname was too babyish, I started calling myself Hal.

My father, Eugene, was a fair-skinned man with straight hair, born of a well-respected Charleston family. His mother, Estelle Baron Jackson, was a slender, very fair mulatto woman who could have passed for White. Neither she nor my father ever made mention of my grandfather. I don't even know his name. All I ever knew of him was that he was a well-to-do White gentleman and that my grandmother bore him three sons and a daughter throughout the course of their relationship.

My mother was dark-complected, and I have been told that she was born to the Reverend and Mrs. James Rivers on James Island, one of the Sea Islands off the South Carolina coast. My mother's people, like most of the Sea Islanders, were descendants of escaped slaves who had sought refuge on the island's isolated shores. That isolation enabled them to retain many of the customs and language forms of their African homeland. As a small child, I remember being fascinated by the cadence of my mother's speech and her glowing, golden brown skin. But there were some people on my father's side of the family who thought that these same attributes were unforgivable flaws. They rarely missed an opportunity to whisper about how my father had married beneath him.

My father was a tailor, and by the time I was born, he had a shop on Society Street across from the Charleston Hotel. His main contract was with the U.S. Navy, making uniforms for the Citadel. The business was lucrative enough for us to afford a house at 18 Charles Street in one of the better Black residential areas of the city. It was an imposing wood-framed house built in traditional Southern style. The ground floor had a porch that wrapped around the entire length of the house. My mother's ferns and bright flowering houseplants covered that porch from end to end. She arranged them on the shelves of a tall, handsomely built plant stand that had been designed especially for her because she wanted the house to have a warm, welcoming look. Both the second and third floors had porches that faced out onto the backyard. We had a stable in the backyard for our horse and surrey. Later, when we became the first Black family in the city to buy an automobile, my father had the stable converted into a garage.

Everything in the house was elegant. On the first floor, there was a living room, back parlor, dining room, and kitchen. The living room, awash in bright reds and yellows, had a love seat, oversized chairs, and antique tables. Showcased in the front of the room was a grand piano that was almost identical to the baby grand piano in the parlor. Plush carpeting and handwoven rugs covered the floors. My parents' bedroom was on the second floor; my two sisters, Esyelee and Alice, also had rooms there. My brothers, Leroy and Eugene, and I had our rooms on the top floor. All day long, servants bustled around the house. We had two maids, a laundry woman, a stable hand, and a cook, who all worked under my mother's careful supervision.

As a child, I never played with the few other children who lived in our middle-class neighborhood. Though my parents never said anything specifically, my brothers and sisters and I got the distinct impression that those other children weren't good enough to be our friends. We never went to public school either because our father didn't approve of the quality of education at the Black public schools. He always told us that all they taught in the Black schools was washing, ironing, cooking, and cleaning, and that was not what we were born for.

To make up for our lack of companionship, we got toys and presents. Any toy you can name, we had. As I recall, my brothers and I played a lot of baseball. My two sisters had instructors come to the house in the afternoons to teach them knitting, crochet, embroidery, and music. In fact, there was always music in my house. My oldest sister Esyelee, whom we all called Essie, attended and graduated from the Boston Conservatory of Music. She was the first Black ever to attend the conservatory. Alice, meanwhile, studied the violin at home.

I was a serious child, and a loner, so my Aunt Lillian would sometimes try to engage me by taking me down to Charleston Harbor, where I would sit on a bench and watch the ships come in. One day, a little goat joined me from out of nowhere and just lay down next to me. I petted it while I watched the ships. When my aunt said it was time to go home, I said "Bye-bye" to the goat and got up to leave. To my surprise and pleasure, the little goat followed me all the way home through the streets of Charleston.

We had a large backyard, and my father allowed me to keep the goat there. In the evening, the goat would climb the stairs to the house and cuddle up on the floor next to my bed. He seemed to love being near me and quickly became very attached. The feeling, of course, was mutual. To me, that little goat was more than just a pet. At that point, he was my only friend. But one day, in the middle of a jealous tantrum, my oldest brother Eugene picked up my goat and dropped it over the banister of the porch outside my bedroom. The goat plunged three flights of stairs to the ground. One of its legs was broken, and my father had to take it to the vet to have the leg splinted. I remember crying and crying and not understanding that kind of senseless cruelty to an innocent animal. My confusion and intense feelings of anger and indignation lingered long after the goat's leg healed.

Not long after that incident, I began attending services at the sanctified church up the street from my house. An old, whitewashed wooden storefront on Charles Street served as the meeting hall. My family was not especially religious; we went to church, Baptist, I think, but I don't remember much about it. It must have been one of the more staid, middle-class congregations that lacked the drama of the storefront church. That sanctified church had services almost every evening, and the whole neighborhood could hear the singing and shouting. The congregation joined in with the choir on almost every song, tambourines jumping and feet stomping, intent on making a joyful noise unto the Lord. Even though I couldn't have been more than 5 or 6 years old at the time, my father gave me permission to go to the services. I would enter that church all by myself, fascinated by the drama and emotion that seemed to engulf the sanctuary.

One of the most enthralling parts of the service was what the church elder called "speaking in an unknown tongue." Everyone would stand up and shout "Jesus, Jesus, Jesus" as fast as they could until it was impossible to understand what they were saying. As the congregation got into the spirit, they would close their eyes, shout, and dance. Once a month, they would wash each other's feet. I don't think I went to that church to fill a spiritual need so much as to be a part of the drama and music the services offered. I've always liked a good show, and those evenings in the sanctified church in my Charleston neighborhood gave me my first pointers in how to put one on. When I was about 6 or 7, the church broke up and everybody went their separate ways. It seems that the elder, whom I had always thought of as a really sharp, hip guy, had gotten himself hooked up with somebody else's wife. The day that the sanctified church closed its doors was the end of an era for me.

My father, always a very thoughtful, kind man, tried as much as possible to help me fill what might have become just a succession of long, lonely hours. Although he worked hard, he made sure to find time for all his children, too. He would take me with him to his shop sometimes, and I would sit on the steps outside and watch the children who attended the White school next door come and go. I had just started attending Avery Normal Institute, which was probably the most outstanding private school for Blacks in the country at that time. But it still did not compare to the White school near my father's shop. I don't remember feeling any resentment or bitterness over that fact—it was just the way things were in those days.

The tailor shop was about twenty or thirty blocks from our house. Located at 63 Society Street, it stood around the corner from Meeting and King Streets, the main thoroughfares in the business district. Because it was quite a distance, I usually rode on the Charleston trolley car with our maid, whom we children called Titer (which was supposed to be short for "Sister"). I loved watching the throngs of people making their way through the crowded streets and alleys. Hawkers and street vendors with horse-drawn carts haggled with passersby and tried to entice the shoppers into buying whatever it was that they had to sell.

Sometimes, in the evenings and on the weekends, I would go to the tailor shop by myself and wait for my father to close up so we could go home together. That was how I met my friend Porgy—coming home from the tailor shop with my father one evening. Porgy had no legs and propelled himself with padded hands on a little cart. Later, he was immortalized in the opera *Porgy and Bess* by George Gershwin. He was a kind, very intelligent man who was never too busy to answer the questions of a 6- or 7-year-old boy.

Porgy lived in a small tenement apartment on Catfish Row. The only entrance was through a back alley. One day, he let me accompany him home. Everybody seemed to know Porgy, calling out to him as he passed by. I was curious about how he had lost his legs, but I never got up the courage to ask him. Porgy himself never seemed to acknowledge that he was handicapped; he acted as if he had two legs, and certainly didn't seem to feel sorry for himself. Looking back, I believe I was influenced by Porgy's outlook on life. Though I couldn't have known it, I was about to go through one of the most difficult periods of my life. But even through the hardest times, like Porgy, I never allowed myself to wallow in self-pity. I always looked to the future.

When I was about 8 years old, my mother developed tuberculosis. Her doctor suggested that my father take her to the Pines. This was what they called the Pinehurst area of North Carolina. At that time, it was believed that pine forest air could cure tuberculosis. Of course, it didn't. I was too young to fully understand what was happening. All I remember is that her illness distracted the entire family.

A few months after her illness was diagnosed, my mother died. Directly on the heels of her sudden death, my father fell ill. He always had high blood pressure, and I suppose the stress of my mother's death aggravated his condition. My sister Essie, who was 21 years old by that time and had just graduated from the Boston Conservatory, rushed home when she heard about my father's condition. So did my sister Alice, who was 18 years old and had also been away at school. But by that point, he was already too far gone. Just four months and twelve days after my mother died, my father died of general complications from his high blood pressure.

After our father passed, we found out that Essie had been named guardian of the entire estate and all of the money. My parents had died with somewhere around $80,000 to $100,000 in assets, which in those days was a lot of money. They had further provided for their children by buying each of us our own home. My father's will stated that the money, jewelry, and houses were to be relinquished to each of us as we came of age. Since Eugene was 16, Leroy was 14, and I was only 8, our homes were held in trust for us under our sister's guardianship. But Essie never told us.

I found out about the houses by accident. Many years later, I came across some old bank documents on which Essie had forged her name, turning the house that my parents had left me over to herself. She sold it, just as she had quietly sold my other siblings' houses, without our knowledge or consent. But, of course, I was a child trying to cope with the death of my parents, and the thought of money never crossed my mind. Although the loss of my father's fortune would affect me greatly a few years down the line, at the time I was just a frightened little boy trying to make it from one day to the next.

Leroy and I stayed with various relatives in Charleston while I finished my last year at Avery Normal. My brother Eugene went to stay with relatives in New York.

During that year, my two sisters and their new husbands vacationed in Europe, living lavishly off the proceeds of our joint inheritance. To this day, I don't know exactly how my parents' money was squandered, but Essie and Alice managed to spend almost all of it during the course of their travels.

Upon their return, Leroy and I joined Eugene in New York, and the three of us went to live with Essie in the Bronx. At the end of the year, Leroy and I went to live with Alice in Washington, D.C. She sent Leroy, who was really her pet, to prep school at Troy Academy in Vermont. When I asked if I could go also, she said no, there wasn't enough money for both of us. The next year, when I was 12, I got into Troy on a full scholarship, but when the year ended so did the scholarship money, and I had to come home. In fact, both my brother and I had to leave the academy, because my sisters couldn't pay for either of us. So I came back to D.C. and enrolled at Banneker Junior High School. Banneker was named for the famous Black clock maker and almanac writer who had helped survey and lay out the nation's capital. Like the other schools in D.C., it was segregated. Though I hadn't welcomed the idea of going to Banneker, once I found myself there I threw myself into my schoolwork, determined to do well.

Meanwhile, things weren't working out well with my sister Alice. She and her husband, Henry Cornish, were a socially active, upwardly mobile young couple living in a middle-class section of the city. Henry was a postal worker—a much sought-after occupation for Blacks at the time—and my sister taught elementary school. Neither of them wanted to be bothered with a ready-made family. Even though nothing was said outright, through subtle actions it became clear to me that my presence was not particularly welcome. So instead of remaining dependent on people whom I felt resented me, I declared my independence and, at the age of 13, moved out on my own.

I rented a room in a boardinghouse on W Street owned by Mrs. Althea Anderson. The room cost $5 a week. I had to find some way to pay it, so I got my first job shining shoes at Union Station. Once I had proved myself serious and dependable, I was offered the opportunity for steadier work—cleaning the latrines. Every morning I would get up at 5 A.M., take the bus to the station, where I would clean lavatories from 6 to 8:30, then I would get back on the bus and be at school by 9 A.M. After school, I worked as a busboy at various White restaurants. There were no regular wages, but I got free meals and tips— roughly $4 or $5 a day, more on Saturdays.

I still found time to go to the library, for books were among my best friends at that point in my life. I loved the quiet stillness of the local Black library, and while I couldn't spend much time there, I had my library card and borrowed books to read at night and on the bus to and from school and my various jobs. My favorite books were biographies of famous people. I wanted to find out what made them special, how they got started, and how they became successful. I wanted to set goals for myself, to be the best I could be. I always felt that nothing was impossible, and reading those biographies supported my feelings.

During this time, I started saving my tips to buy my first Emerson radio receiver. From the moment I acquired that set, radio was my main form of entertainment and information. There were no Black radio stations and no programs by Blacks in those days, with the exception of the weekly religious broadcast from Griffith Stadium by Elder Solomon Lightfoot Micheaux. He was the Billy Graham of the time and would draw as many as 40,000 spectators to his baptismal services at the stadium—people of all colors and walks of life. Micheaux was a handsome, impeccably dressed, light-skinned man with the power and influence of a Martin Luther King and the elegance of a Sidney Poitier. Even President John Calvin Coolidge attended those meetings. Elder Micheaux's brother was the pioneering Black filmmaker Oscar Micheaux, so I guess showmanship ran in the family. Whenever I could, I went to those Griffith Stadium services. But when I couldn't, I listened to the live broadcast over Washington's largest radio station, WTOP.

When I wasn't listening to Elder Micheaux's religious meetings, my radio was constantly tuned to sports broadcasts. In fact, it would probably be fair to say that my love of sports began to dominate my life. It had started a couple of years before, right around the time that I first arrived in Washington. My sister would let me go up to Howard University and hang out with the football players, and they befriended me. Ultimately I became the mascot of the Howard University football and basketball teams, and I'd lead them out to the floor. It thrilled me to be close to the action whenever and wherever I could.

Only White games were broadcast on the radio in those days, but that didn't matter to me. I just wanted to listen to games—I didn't care who was playing. Washington, D.C., had its own baseball team, the Senators, who played at Griffith Stadium. I couldn't afford a ticket, but I would hang around the stadium anyway, just to soak up the atmosphere. Although I felt somewhat conspicuous—there didn't seem to be any Black people around—I was determined to be part of that world, so I watched and waited until I discovered where Mr. Clark Griffith, the owner of the stadium, had his office. After that, I started hanging around there. One day when he stepped outside for a breath of fresh air, I walked right up to him and asked if he would let me watch the games in exchange for picking up the trash in the stadium during game time. He agreed, and after that I spent a lot of time at Griffith Stadium, cleaning up trash and watching the games. The players got used to seeing me around and accepted me as part of the maintenance crew.

My most thrilling experience at that time was when Babe Ruth gave me a ride home in his car one afternoon. The Yankees had just played the Senators and everyone was packing up and getting ready to go home. I lived ten or twelve blocks from the stadium on Second Street. I was just about to leave the stadium and walk home when the Babe came up to me and asked if I'd like a ride. Of course I said yes, and we hopped into his chauffeur-driven limousine and took off. We talked a bit along the way. He asked me questions about school and whether or

not I played sports. I told him that I loved baseball and that I was a left-handed first baseman.

"Usually those guys are pretty tall," he said. "You ever think about playing any other positions?"

I said, "Maybe, but I'm left-handed and I think it's great that I'm able to deliver in that position."

Deferring to my obvious 13-year-old expertise, he smiled and dropped the issue. The thing I remember most clearly about the Babe is that he was such a classy man, not at all like the crass womanizer and drunkard that so many people like to portray him as. His offer to drop me off was an act of kindness I never forgot.

Not all of my memories from my Griffith Stadium days are as wonderful. Occasionally, I'd volunteer to do errands for the players. One particularly hot afternoon, the great Senators catcher Muddy Rule wanted a soda and I volunteered to get it for him.

I yelled over to him, "Hey, Muddy, what kinda soda do you want?"

One of the other players, a bigoted redneck, jumped up and roared at me, "Look, nigger, as long as you live, don't you ever call him Muddy."

"What did you say?" I asked him.

He said, "You heard me. Don't you ever call that White man Muddy. It's Mr. Rule to you!"

One of the other players immediately got up and cursed him out for talking that way to a little kid. But I learned an important lesson that day. I realized that there would always be people like him trying to degrade me and tell me who I was and what I could or could not do. And there wouldn't always be someone else around to stand up and defend me. It was up to me to make sure that I knew how to handle those people so that they never became stumbling blocks in my path.

I struggled to make it on my own for another two years. Then, when I turned 15, I decided to travel to New York to confront my sister Essie. No one had ever explained to me what happened to our parents money and I didn't understand why they would allow a 15-year-old boy to work two, sometimes three jobs (not including my time at the stadium) to support himself while going to school full-time. So I took a bus to New York and showed up on Essie's doorstep. I don't know whether she was unwilling or unable to tell me the things I wanted to know, but I left her home without any of the answers I sought.

Distraught, I wandered around the unfamiliar streets of the Bronx trying to figure out what to do. I was in a strange city with no money and nowhere to live. But figuring that I had nothing left to lose, I decided to stay in New York and take my chances. I slept in subway stations for a time. When I found a job, I used the money to rent a $5-a-week room—and quickly discovered that $5 didn't go nearly as far in New York as it did in Washington. I don't remember much more about that time. I enrolled at DeWitt Clinton High School in the Bronx and stayed there a semester before realizing that I needed to be close to my family. After about six months, I packed it in and moved back to Washington.

I could have quit school, but education was important to

me. I enrolled at Dunbar High School, the most famous of Washington's three Black high schools, because of Charles Pendahughes, the football coach. Coach Pendahughes wanted me on his football team, and I played on that team all four years. But I loved all sports, not just football. Before long, I was a five-letter guy—football, baseball, basketball, track, and tennis teams. I changed my weekday work schedule so I would have the afternoons for practice and didn't have to start my restaurant jobs until after 6 P.M. I think my favorite sport was baseball. I was first baseman on the all–high school team three years. Between my sports schedule and my work schedule, I stayed really busy.

I also got my first job in the entertainment business while I was at Dunbar. On Friday and Saturday nights, I went to the Masonic Temple, where they had dances for high school kids. I wasn't much for dancing, but I enjoyed the professional band that provided the music and would sit up on stage with them when I had the chance. I got to know the band members and a lot of the numbers in their repertoire. One night the bandleader handed me his megaphone and said, "Why don't you sing with us?" I was nervous, but I must have done all right, because I was hired to perform with them every weekend. But that career was short-lived. I was more interested in sports than singing.

I soon discovered that the best thing about the baseball games was not the action on the field but the action in the broadcast booth. From there, high above the diamond, a broadcaster named Arch McDonald provided game coverage for the radio audience. Observing the way Arch worked, I realized that this was what I wanted to do: broadcast baseball games on the radio.

If I had confided my dream to anyone, I would probably have been told it was impossible. Blacks weren't allowed to do anything in Washington, D.C. But I was a dreamer and a doer, and I figured there must be a way. Like my friend Porgy back in Charleston, I never dwelt on what I couldn't do; I just went out and did it.

2.

MARRIAGE, SPORTSWRITING, AND BROADCASTING

*I*n spite of all my activities, I did well at Dunbar High School and managed to graduate a semester early, in February instead of June, 1933. At age 17, I enrolled as a nonmatriculating student at Howard University, taking courses in physical education. I did not have the money to go full-time. The country was deep in the Depression, and like millions of other Americans, I had to struggle to make ends meet.

The university had been founded as Howard Seminary in 1867 by the American Missionary Society. The idea was to give Blacks in the post–Civil War period a chance to pursue higher education. Over the years, Howard became a mainstay of Washington's Black community. In addition to offering courses in a range of subjects, it provided us with organized sports. The theater arts program, with its Howard Players, gave talented young people a chance to learn acting and staging skills.

At the time I entered, Howard was not the great academic institution it would later become. Most of the faculty were part-time, and many were White; most of the students went part-time as well because they had to work regular jobs. But things were starting to change. A few years earlier, the president, Mordecai Johnson, had decided to make Howard University Law School the "West Point of Negro Leadership." Charles Hamilton Houston, the newly appointed vice dean, started hiring full-time and Black faculty to teach courses that focused on how existing laws could be made to work for Black people. Thurgood Marshall graduated from Howard University Law School in 1933.

I had not been at Howard long when I decided to get married to my high school sweetheart, Claudia Parrat. Claudia was one of the sweetest, most generous girls I had ever known. We had met at Dunbar, and over time we fell in love. In those days, if you were in love, you got married. The legal age for men to marry in Washington was 21, and I was only 18 years old (Claudia also was only 18). We must have visited four different justices of the peace in neighboring Maryland and Virginia before we found one who would overlook my immaturity and marry us. Looking back I marvel at my youthful enthusiasm. There I was, 18 years old, in the midst of the Great Depression, and married.

Claudia and I moved into a tiny apartment on the corner of Second and W Streets, and I immediately began looking for a better-paying job. To add to the stress placed on our young marriage, we found out about a year later that Claudia was pregnant. Between school and work, I began spending less and less time with my wife and the separation took its toll. Just a few months before the birth of our child, Claudia moved out of our apartment, and I filed for divorce.

On September 4, 1936, our daughter Jane was born. Two months later, exactly six days after my twenty-first birthday, I got served with the papers stating that my marriage had officially been dissolved. Our divorce was final.

Claudia had no family to speak of and no way to support the baby, so we decided that it would be best for everyone involved if I took sole responsibility for Jane. But after the decision had been made, I had to admit to myself that I didn't have many more resources than Claudia. With no one else to watch her, I took Jane with me wherever I went. When I went to basketball games, I carried her with me in a makeshift backpack. It wasn't unusual to see me, or even some of the players who were my friends, changing diapers on the bench at halftime. Sometimes I carried her zipped up inside my jacket. I was a devoted father—and mother—to my child and I loved it.

In spite of all of my responsibilities, or perhaps because of them, I was more determined than ever to continue with my education. Because I had to take care of Jane and work during the day, the only time I could find to attend classes was at night. It was in one of these night classes that I met a beautiful young woman from Baltimore named Julia Hawkins. I noticed Julia right off because her face and figure reminded me (and every other guy in our class) of Lena Horne, a gorgeous young star with whom we were all captivated at the time. Many years later Julia told me that she fell in love with me after seeing how gentle and devoted I was to Jane. Whatever the reason, Julia and I fell in love and soon became inseparable. We were married early in 1938.

Suddenly, however, I found myself responsible not only for my bride, my baby daughter, and myself but also for my mother-in-law, Mrs. Ercer Iola Ricks. Julia and I in moved into a house at 5302 East Capitol Street. Never one to mince words, Ercer let it be known that she thought I should do better by her daughter. But that was easier said than done. The Depression had cast its shadow over Washington, just as it had over the rest of the country, and Blacks, always last hired and first fired, had it as bad as it could be. The long lines at soup kitchens in the Black community, and the piles of belongings in the streets from the latest evictions, were just a small part of the story.

In addition to working full-time to support my family, I was still pursuing my interest in sports. At Howard, I continued to be involved with the players on the various teams and to function as an unofficial assistant manager, having "graduated" from my role as mascot. I still went to Griffith Stadium every chance I got so that I could watch the games and hang around with Sam Lacey.

Sam was the national sports editor for *The Afro-American* newspaper chain, which had a national edition as well as local editions published twice a week out of Washington, Baltimore, New York, and Philadelphia. Sam also did the play-by-play for the Black sports events at Griffith Stadium. Black teams played at the stadium when the White teams were out of town. How well I remember watching the great Negro League teams, like the Kansas City Monarchs and the Washington Homestead Grays, and befriending the great Black stars, like Satchel Paige, Josh Gibson, and Jackie Robinson, who started out with the Kansas City Monarchs.

I remember once when Jackie Robinson called me up and told me that he was getting ready to quit baseball. He said it was too hard playing in the Negro Leagues. The players never got a break. It was a common thing to play a game in the afternoon, get in a bus, travel to wherever you had to be, and then play a game that night. Then you might have to ride all night and play the next day. Jackie said he didn't see any future in it, so he was getting ready to take over as the head of a YMCA in Dallas, Texas. I tried to encourage him to hold on to his dream of playing in the major leagues, but he was very depressed because he thought that it was never going to happen. Thankfully, he hung in there and went on to make baseball history.

Josh Gibson was another baseball great that I became close to during my time at Griffith Stadium. Josh was a lot of fun. He acted like a big kid, always playing jokes on people. He would do things like hide some of the guys' uniforms and then come in wearing them. I was there when the Grays went to New York to play the Yankees and Josh hit the longest home run that has ever been hit in Yankee Stadium. Right out of the park. It must have gone fifteen blocks away from the stadium.

The White baseball games would attract 3,000 or 4,000 fans to Griffith Stadium, but when the Black teams played, 32,000 people would pack that arena. Of course, when a team like the Washington Senators played, the game was broadcast over the radio, so people could stay at home and listen to them.

The Black games were never broadcast, but there was play-by-play announcing from the broadcast booth, and Sam Lacey did that.

I met Sam while I was in high school, and he became a real mentor to me. He watched me play ball and talked to me for hours about sports. After I graduated from high school, he used to take me along to some of the sports events he covered. I especially remember going to boxing matches; usually, Sam and I were the only Blacks at ringside. After a while, he must have decided that I knew enough about sports to report on them, and he helped me get a job as sports editor for the Washington *Afro-American*. I covered all the local sports events, especially high school and college games. I loved that job, writing about what mattered most to me, and I kept at it for about ten years before my other activities made it impossible. Blacks loved sports as much as Whites, and my coverage of the Washington sports scene soon made my name well-known in the Black community. I started being asked to emcee at benefits and make appearances as a local celebrity.

Besides announcing at the Black baseball games at Griffith Stadium, Sam Lacey lined up the Black teams who played when the White teams weren't playing. I'd hang around the booth as often as I could and talk sports with Sam. I guess it was during those talks that he realized I had a good, deep voice for announcing. One day when I was in the booth with him, he handed me the mike.

"Come on, you can do it," said Sam. He made sure I knew how to turn the mike on and off, and then I was on my own. Of course, I had listened to Sam announce the play-by-play lots of times, and I knew the game and the players inside out, so I wasn't unprepared. I welcomed the teams, talked about the lineups, and gave the stats on each player as he came up at bat. It was a lot of fun. Soon, I was also doing the announcing at the games over at Howard University.

But no one heard me except the audiences in the stadiums, because Black sports competitions still weren't broadcast over the radio. I thought they should be. I talked to Sam about it, but he didn't think there was anything we could do to change things in that segregated town. Still, I wanted to try.

One day soon afterward, I went down to Eighth and I Streets NW, to WINX, a station owned by *The Washington Post*, the biggest newspaper in the city. I knew the station manager was a real redneck, so I didn't even try to make an advance appointment. I just walked into the station and told the receptionist I wanted to see the guy who ran the station.

When she asked what I wanted to see him about, I said, "I'm the announcer at Griffith Stadium, and I want to talk to him about a special program." She sent me right in.

The general manager was interested in the idea, so I told him I would be willing to buy the time and sell it to advertisers. But, then he told me he was interested only if it was done his way. "*I'll* get the announcer for the games," he said.

When I made it clear that I was planning to do the announcing, he wanted to know what training I'd had. I told him I'd trained myself, but that really wasn't what he was getting at. He finally came out with it, "No nigger will ever go on this radio station."

It was about 5 o'clock in the afternoon. He called his whole staff in, and he said to them, "I brought you all in here because, can you imagine, this nigger is talking about going on this radio station." He just lay back and laughed. "No nigger will ever go on this radio station."

"Well, we'll see about that," I said, and walked out.

I left the station hopping mad but determined that this was just the first skirmish in a battle I intended to win.

Sam Lacey had been right—I would get nowhere trying to do sports broadcasts. But by this time I was ready to broadcast any kind of show, on principal. The only kinds of radio shows that featured Black people were religious shows. I knew that there was a market for other types of shows and that regardless of the manager's personal prejudices, a radio station was basically interested in only one color—green. If I couldn't sell a program idea because I was Black, I might still be able to buy airtime through the sales department and avoid the general manager altogether.

I needed a sponsor, and I found him in C. C. Coley, who owned five or six barbecue restaurants around town, including one near Howard University and another at Ninth and U Streets called the Hollywood Grill. I told C. C. about my meeting with the station manager of WINX and of my plan to maneuver around him if C. C. would agree to sponsor a nightly program.

"What would you do on the show?" C. C. wanted to know.

"Let's call it *The Bronze Review*," I said. "This will let Black people know it's a Black program. I'll get the *Afro* to promote it. Let's buy time across the board, Monday through Saturday, through a White advertising agency. That way, the station won't know what's going on the air until after the contract is signed."

C.C. was willing to back me. He contacted a White advertising agency he'd done business with before, Cal Ehrlich and Merrick. The agency had no problem being a front for our cause—not out of any sympathy for Black people but because the proposal made good business sense to them. They could see the potential of the Black market in Washington and wanted to position themselves to take advantage of the situation.

Through Cal Ehrlich and Merrick, we had to submit an outline for the show. The presentation we put together made no mention of the color of the proposed participants. All it said was that this would be a nightly program of live entertainment, interviews, and news. Whites in D.C. were so unaware of the Black community that the title, *The Bronze Review*, didn't tip off anyone at the station, although we knew people in the Black community would catch on right away that it was for them.

The proposal was accepted, and Cal Ehrlich bought fifteen minutes of air time on WINX six nights a week for $35 per show. The time slot we were able to get, 11 to 11:15 P.M., was not exactly prime time, but we knew we could get the listeners at any time of the day or night for this historic "first."

Then I got busy promoting the show; it was about the easiest promotional job I've ever had. This was big—the first show of its kind, produced by Blacks for Blacks, in Washington. I used every Black medium at my disposal to let people know what was about to happen. The *Afro* gave me advance publicity with big headlines. I personally distributed handbills all over the community, including C. C. Coley's barbecue restaurants and Abe Lichtman's theaters. I even drove around the Black business district on Seventh Street NW, with a PA system on the car roof, announcing that *The Bronze Review* was coming.

Even with all that promotion, the people at WINX, the city's third largest radio station, owned by the biggest newspaper, the *Washington Post*, never caught on. The White establishment never paid Black people any mind in those days. They had no Black employees, except maybe janitors; they didn't read the Black newspapers; there weren't any Black radio programs. They were blissfully ignorant of what was going on in the Black community.

While I was busy promoting the new show, I was lining up guests. For my first guest, I chose Dr. Mary McLeod Bethune, one of the best known—if not *the* best known—Black woman of that time. Dr. Bethune, who had founded Bethune-Cookman College in Daytona Beach, Florida, was the first African American to hold high office in the U.S. government. In 1936, President Roosevelt appointed her director of the Division of Negro Affairs within the newly established National Youth Administration. Later, when the United States started gearing up for World War II, President Roosevelt appointed her head of the Resident War Production Training Center in Wilberforce, Ohio. He also set up an Office of Minority Affairs, which she administered. She was great friends with Mrs. Eleanor Roosevelt, and many a night when I was with her, she would call the First Lady at the White House just to talk.

I first got to know Mrs. Bethune when she was trying to raise money to move the National Council of Negro Women into a new office on Vermont Avenue. I suggested that we do a series of benefit baseball games at Griffith Stadium. We put on a series of about four games that paid for the renovation of the organization's new national headquarters. So when I asked her to be my first guest, she was pleased to say yes.

The Bronze Review premiered in November 1939. I arrived with Mrs. Bethune just fifteen minutes before airtime that first night. The racist general manager of the station was gone for the day, and the shocked WINX staff who were there didn't know what to do. They tried calling the manager, but I don't

Famed educator and founder of the National Council of Negro Women Dr. Mary McLeod Bethune and Hal, 1940s

think they reached him. Anyway, it was so close to airtime that there really wasn't anything they could do but let me go on.

At 11 P.M., the red light lit up, and we were on the air. We didn't have any script, but I had a good sense of what our listeners wanted to hear. Dr. Bethune and I talked about her work on behalf of Black people, especially Black women, and about her friendship with the Roosevelts. She was very concerned about the lack of jobs in the Black community. She also talked about some of the projects that she was working on with Mrs. Eleanor Roosevelt. I had actually met Mrs. Roosevelt through Dr. Bethune, and we discussed the times that the three of us rode through some of the most blighted, poverty-stricken neighborhoods in Washington because Mrs. Roosevelt wanted to get out and meet the people personally. She wanted to hear directly from their own mouths about their major concerns and problems and how the New Deal policies were affecting their lives. The show went beautifully.

We were hardly off the air when the phones at the station started ringing. Not one caller complained about a Black show being on the air. Everyone who called said what a terrific show it was and praised the Graham family, who owned *The Washington Post* and WINX, for initiating this great concept. Faced with this overwhelmingly positive reaction, the Grahams were hardly going to pull the show off the air.

While I was thrilled with the reception that *The Bronze Review* received from the community, something even more wonderful happened in my life just a few weeks later. Julia gave birth to our son, Harold Jackson Jr., in December 1939. We nicknamed the baby Jacky. His arrival in our family was a blessing that renewed my faith in the future. Nothing was too tough to overcome. Looking back, I marvel at my youthful enthusiasm. Even though the responsibilities kept piling up, I was young and strong and I thought I could handle anything.

The Bronze Review stayed on the air for about two years. During that time many famous people were my guests. I interviewed Lena Horne, Dr. Mordecai Johnson, president of Howard University, and J. Raymond Jones, the powerful Democratic district leader from Harlem. When he was in his heyday as congressman from Harlem, Adam Clayton Powell Jr. also made several appearances on my show, and we developed a great friendship. Adam was always flamboyant, charismatic, and aggressive. He would come by and pick me up at the station, and we would go to different restaurants that accepted all of the other members of Congress but excluded Blacks. Adam, who was from New York, refused to let the rules of segregation prevent him from doing anything he wanted to do. He would look at me and say, "Come on, let's go, Hal," and walk right in. Nobody dared to stop him. Whenever I came to New York, I stopped by the Abyssinian Baptist Church to visit with him. He kept Abyssinian open seven days and nights a week for anybody who had a problem with housing, food, or anything else. Adam really took care of the people.

Others, like Walter White of the NAACP, Whitney Young of the National Urban League, and John H. Johnson, the energetic young publisher of a magazine called *The Negro Digest*, were guests of mine as well. John Johnson's interview stands out in my mind because of what happened after we got off the air. Once the show was over, he and I got to talking. He told me that he was going to start a new magazine called *Ebony*. It was during the war, so many supplies were being rationed. He had to get permission from the War Department to get paper to put the magazine out. I went to the War Department with him and two or three other people to make the plea, and, boy, were they rough! The first thing they said was, "What are you going to do with this magazine?"

"We are going to use *Ebony* magazine to lift the morale of the Black soldier because our soldiers have nothing to look forward to," I said. "They need this magazine! That's why you should give us an allotment of paper." We got the paper, and *Ebony* magazine went on to become one of the most widely circulated Black magazines in the country.

One of my favorite guests was Dr. Charles Drew, who discovered blood plasma. He came on the show quite a few times, and each time we'd reminisce about Dunbar High School, which he had also attended. He'd gone there about ten years before me, and he, too, had lettered in baseball, basketball, football, and track. Early in World War II, Dr. Drew had set up a blood bank in England. When the United States entered the war, in 1941, he went to work for the National Research Council, in charge of collecting blood for the U.S. Army and Navy. As a scientist he knew that there was no difference between White and Black blood, and when the army and navy started refusing colored blood donors because some Whites didn't want their sons or brothers receiving blood from Black people, Dr. Drew resigned from the program.

Soon after one of his appearances on the show, Charles had a car accident while he was driving South to a reunion at

*Hal with Dr. Charles Drew, who discovered blood plasma,
after a* **WINX** *interview, 1940*

Tuskegee. None of the White hospitals would take him in, and, unable to find a Black hospital or doctor to treat him in time, he bled to death. The irony of the creator of blood plasma bleeding to death on a dark country road just because of the color of his skin affected me so deeply that even now, more than 50 years later, I still grieve for the loss of that great mind.

Once the radio barrier for Blacks was broken in D.C., things happened very quickly. The Seventh Street merchants banded together and bought time on WINX for a music show, with me as host. They built entire promotional campaigns around the show, advertising some piece of merchandise and announcing that Hal Jackson would be at the store: "Come get Hal's autograph and let him show you this product himself!" I was becoming a drawing card, a VIP.

Earlier in the year, the *Chicago Defender* sponsored a round-trip flight from Chicago to Washington, D.C., by members of Cornelius Coffey's all-Black National Airmen's Association. The trip was intended to dramatize the importance of opening aviation to African Americans and to press for more government support of Black aviation. Seeing a chance to help break down a major barrier, I was inspired to get private pilot training in Virginia. After President Roosevelt ordered the War Department to create a Black flying unit as part of the U.S. Army Air Corps (this was before the air force was set up as a separate branch of the armed services), I thought I had a chance to join the corps. I volunteered to be part of the training program that became known as the Tuskegee Airmen, but I was turned down. The army chose only the cream of the crop—men from active army artillery units, policemen, and men with advanced college degrees.

The government had its own plans for my contribution to the war effort, however. The Department of Health established a program to identify carriers of disease in the Black community. The program was based on the dubious assumption that Blacks had a higher rate of disease than Whites. The fear was that this high incidence of disease would hamper the war effort now that more Blacks were being allowed into the military. Because of my popularity and recognition in Washington's Black community, I was asked to help health officials track down carriers of polio, tuberculosis, and venereal disease and bring them in for treatment. So that's how I served my country during World War II.

They called this program the Tuskegee Experiment. My

role was to track down young women who had been listed by soldiers as the source of a venereal disease and inform them that they needed to come in for an examination immediately. I didn't want to embarrass anyone, so I would make up some excuse to get the girls by themselves, away from family and friends, and then let them know what my visit was really about. I would show them the form that said "You have been named by Sergeant So-and-so as infecting him with a veneral disease. You must come in for an examination." I didn't find out about the *other* Tuskegee Experiment, in which Black soldiers with syphilis were deliberately denied treatment and lied to, until much, much later.

Still, I held out hopes of getting into the air corps. By 1940, the United States was gearing up for war, and it looked as if there might be more chances for Blacks in the armed services. Aviation had taken on great importance in the war in Europe, and U.S. manufacture of war planes had become a national priority. So was training pilots to fly them. A program called the Civilian Pilot Training Program had been started a couple of years before, and under pressure from the NAACP the program started to admit Blacks. But my superiors at the Department of Health sent a letter to the War Department saying that I should not be considered as a candidate for armed service because I was necessary for the war effort in Washington.

As anxious as I was to serve my country overseas, I must admit that staying in Washington afforded me many opportunities to advance my career. First of all, *The Bronze Review* was still on the air and going strong. In fact, I was on the air with the great boxer Joe Louis when the Japanese attacked Pearl Harbor on December 7, 1941. What a shock that was to everyone. Dorie Miller, a Black steward on the USS *West Virginia*, earned the Navy Cross for his heroism that day. He took over a machine gun, which he had not been trained to operate, and destroyed two Japanese aircraft. But even though a Black sailor was one of the first Americans to display heroism in action, Blacks would have a hard time earning the right to serve their country in combat in that war.

Roosevelt's New Deal was putting people back to work, and Works Progress Administration (WPA) construction projects had sprung up all over Washington. I noticed all the piles of dirt and decided to go into the dirt-hauling business. With a friend, John Wallace, I put a down payment on a dump truck and started going to all the construction sites, offering to haul away the dirt. John and I kept that business going for about three years.

Finally, I was able to achieve my original goal of broadcasting the Black baseball games. Through Cal Ehrlich, the White advertising agency that helped us launch *The Bronze Review*, the Negro National League and the Negro American League signed a contract with WINX that enabled their games to be broadcast from Griffith Stadium. WINX would preempt its regular programming whenever Negro League teams came to town. The broadcast announcer was none other than Hal Jackson.

For about two years, I did the play-by-play whenever the Negro League teams played, and as I expected, these shows were the most popular radio shows in the Black community. Soon, another long-held dream of mine came true. With the help of heavyweight sponsors like Philip Morris and Lincoln-Mercury, I finally managed to get the Howard University football games on the air, broadcasting from the Professional Turner Arena. These broadcasts were also big in the Black community and soon had more sponsors than they could handle. I still have a telegram that was sent to the Cavalier Men's Shop on Seventh Street, from a Sergeant Robert Harris at Walter Reed General Hospital.

Telegram from wounded veterans at Walter Reed Hospital in Washington, D.C., thanking Hal for his sports broadcasts, 1945

AS INJURED VETERANS WHO ARE UNABLE TO SEE BALLGAMES MAY WE THANK YOU FOR BROADCASTING HOWARD UNIVERSITY GAMES.

By the time my youngest daughter Jewell was born in August of 1945, I was on the air every day, sometimes several times a day, in different capacities on WINX. It was sweet justice for me, considering that just a few years earlier, WINX had told me that "No nigger will ever go on this radio station."

To The New CARR'S Beach

SUNDAY, AUGUST 27
IVORY JOE HUNTER
AND HIS ORCHESTRA

FRIDAY NITE
AUG. 25 — 10 P. M. TIL ?

HAL JACKSON
and his
HOUSE THAT JACK BUILT
TALENT SHOW

Broadcast 11:30-11:55
Station WNAV
ANNAPOLIS, MD.

plus

DANCING AND PROFESSIONAL SHOW 10 P. M.-2 A. M.

The New . . .
CARR'S BEACH
ANNAPOL

3.

SPORTS PROMOTION AND THE BASKETBALL WORLD CHAMPIONSHIP

I have never been a person to do just one thing at a time. I like to have a lot of irons in the fire. During the war years, while covering sports events for the Washington *Afro-American*, announcing the games at Griffith Stadium and Howard University, broadcasting over WINX, and tracking down carriers of disease for the government, I also got into sports promotion. The war years presented an opportunity to build up sports in Washington, D.C. The district did not have an independent professional basketball team, and I thought it should. Sam Lacey had handed over the announcing at the Black baseball games to me, but the baseball season was short, and I wanted to do more announcing. Sam and I began toying with the idea of getting Blacks involved in basketball during the winter season.

To back up a bit, basketball was another game that was segregated. When the first pro league, the American Basketball League (ABL) was organized in 1925, no Black teams were invited to join, even though—or maybe because—they probably

DJ Hoppy Adams of WANN *Annapolis, Hal, and saxaphonist Illinois Jaquet broadcasting from Carrs Beach, Annapolis, Maryland, 1940s*

had the greatest talents. The same thing happened in 1937 after the ABL folded and the National Basketball League (NBL) was formed—no Black players allowed. Of course, they would play against you, but you couldn't play on the same team with them.

One of the best Black teams was the Rens out of New York. They started out as the Spartan Braves of Brooklyn and later became the Spartan Five. Still later, in 1923, they changed their name to the New York Renaissance, after the Renaissance Ballroom on Seventh Avenue and 138th Street in Harlem, where they played.

The Rens were established before the Harlem Globetrotters formed a team in 1927. The Globetrotters added to the excitement of Black basketball because they became real competition for the Rens. Even more exciting were the games between Black and White clubs. The rivalry between the Rens and the New York Celtics, a White team, was legendary, especially after the Rens won their first world professional championship at Chicago Stadium against the Celtics in 1932.

In 1939, the Rens won their second world championship at Chicago Stadium, but that was their last good year. The Harlem Globetrotters beat them out in the world championship semifinals in 1940. I don't know if the fault lay with management, increased competition from teams like the Globetrotters, or the war, but the Rens broke up after that. Many of the guys went to work for Grumman Aircraft on Long Island, gaining exemption from the military draft in the process.

I saw a chance to put together a team in D.C. with some of the old Rens players as its core. Sam was skeptical when I first broached the idea, but the players I contacted were interested. I've never been one to let a few obstacles get in my way, so I made my first venture into big-time promotion.

The first hurdle was finding an arena for the games. Washington was still a very restrictive town. We used to say during the war that the German POWs had access to more places in downtown Washington than the Black GIs. Blacks weren't allowed to play at Uline Arena. In fact, we weren't even admitted as spectators, and since it was the only facility big enough to accommodate ice shows, that was one form of entertainment that Blacks had to forego altogether. Finally I found a place called Turner's Arena. It was pretty booked up: wrestling every Monday night, boxing on Tuesdays, and other sporting events on Wednesdays through Saturdays—Sunday afternoons were free. That was a good time for us, because so many of the guys were working in New York during the week.

So I took some guys down to see the owner, Joe Turner, who was White. I wanted to show him that he had enough room in there to have a legitimate basketball court. I had somebody mark it off and show him how it could be done, and Joe jumped at it. He promised me that I could have the arena for basketball on Sunday afternoons if I could come up with the money to rent it.

Sometime later, I started the first CIAA (Colored, later Central, Intercollegiate Athletic Association) basketball tournament at Turner's Arena, with Howard University as the host. All the colored teams would come in there and play.

My next step was to assemble a team so I could approach potential sponsors. Recruiting the players was the easiest part. With the White teams off-limits, Black players had few opportunities to play after college. I was able to sign up some talented young players from Howard University and Union College in Richmond, Virginia, and we decided to call the team the Washington Bears.

I also got many of the players from the disbanded Rens. In fact, so many of the players came from the Renaissance that a lot of books on basketball history refer to the Bears as "the former Rens." Most of our guys had grown up around New York. One of our most promising stars, a young man named Wilmeth Sidat-Singh, had even gone to my old high school, DeWitt

Clinton, in New York City. Sidat was phenomenal. He could play a football game in the afternoon and a basketball game at night. He even made All-American in college at Syracuse University. Grantland Rice, a syndicated columnist and one of the best-known sportswriters of the day, wrote a poem about Sidat that described him running down a football field for a touchdown. It went "Did you see that thing? That was Sidat-Singh. The Syracuse walking dream." After graduation, Sidat played with the Syracuse Reds. He led the Rochester Seagrams to the world championship tournament in 1940 and then for a short time played with the Rens before moving to Washington and joining our team.

Sidat was accepted to the Army Air Corps Flying School at Tuskegee and became a member of the 332nd Fighter Group stationed at Selfridge Field, Michigan. But he still played with the Bears every chance he got, coming in for the games from wherever he happened to be. Sadly, he was killed in 1943 when his military plane caught fire and crashed in Lake Huron. Joe Louis had been one of Sidat's friends and admirers, so together, we organized a program in commemoration of Sidat-Singh.

Another guy, Wylie "Soupy" Campbell, was from Richmond. He played on the Virginia Union "dream team" of 1939–1940 that won the CIAA title in 1939. This was one of the first Black college teams to play against a White school, trouncing Brooklyn College 54–38. Clarence "Puggy" Bell, who came down from New York, was a former Ren. We also had William "Dolly" King, who had been a brilliant player at Long Island University. At Alexander Hamilton High School in Brooklyn, he had lettered in baseball, football, and basketball.

In 1937, playing on an integrated team at LIU, he was the first Black player in the national AAU tournament. Two years later, he scored another first when he played for both LIU's basketball and football teams in the same day. After graduating, he played for the Scranton, Pennsylvania, Miners and the Rens.

William "Pops" Gates was another former Ren. He had been with the great Clark College team of 1939. Johnny Isaacs had led the Rens to their great victory over the New York Celtics in 1935. Zack Clayton had worn the jerseys of both the Rens and the Globetrotters at one point and had been on both clubs' world championship teams. Charles "Tarzan" Cooper, from Philadelphia, had been on the Rens' world championship squad in 1939. I got him for a playing coach; I knew he would be able to mold the guys together as a team.

The last hurdle was finding a team sponsor. I was counting on the gate to pay visiting teams and our own team, once we got started. But we needed seed money to pay for uniforms, travel expenses, advertising, and so on. I looked around for a wealthy man with ties to the Black community and an eye for advertising, and it didn't take me long to come up with a name: Abe Lichtman. Abe had seen the profit potential in serving the Black community, and he already owned ten theaters in Washington, D.C., including the famous Howard Theater on T Street. In much of the South, Blacks had to sit in the balcony of "White" theaters; in Washington, we had our own theaters, courtesy of Abe Lichtman.

I didn't know Abe well, but I had met him through my friend Ewell Conway, who did all the marquees for Lichtman's theaters. From hanging out with Ewell, I knew Abe was a great sports fan, so I mentioned to him my idea for a Black basketball team for Washington, and my need for investment capital. Abe didn't need much persuading. "All right," he said, "I'll back you with money for uniforms and whatever else you need, if you put my name on the jerseys." He also offered to advertise the Sunday games at his theaters, right on the screen.

I started bringing in the players, from New York, Philadelphia, and elsewhere to play every Sunday afternoon. A lot of people didn't think the Bears had a chance, but Abe's promotions of the games at his theaters really paid off. I was reporting on the games for the Washington *Afro-American*, and by this time I was also doing a show on WOOK radio, so I talked up the games on that show. Soon, I got the go-ahead to broadcast those Sunday afternoon games from Turner's Arena over WOOK. We filled the arena every time.

The audience was integrated, and everybody was there. Ahmet Ertegun, the music producer, came every Sunday. We mostly played White teams from the NBL, but we also played against local White teams. I remember playing games against Norfolk Naval Training Station. The guy who used to bring the team up there was named Red Auerbach. Red was a phenomenal player, and I could tell from the way that he related to his players that he was a natural coach as well. He could do it all. More importantly, Red seemed to be a genuinely decent guy. He didn't care about color. He was down to hang out with the Black cats on and off the court—not like some other phonies I had encountered. In the service, he had an integrated team.

A little while after Red and I started playing against each other, Mike Uline, owner of the Washington Caps, told me that he was starting a team but he didn't have a coach. I recommended Red for the position and then I called Red and told him to come to Washington. He came up from the training station, talked to Uline, and landed the job. That's how Red Auerbach got his start coaching professional basketball.

Our players worked incredibly hard to keep up with the demands of our schedule. Sometimes we'd play two games a day—one in Washington and then one in Baltimore. During the week, the guys would play up in Rochester and Fort Wayne. Tarzan Cooper did a marvelous job with the players. He was the best. We racked up win after win; we beat all the White teams we played and were the talk of the town, even the country. In the 1942–1943 season, we had a perfect record of 66–0.

With that kind of record, I thought the Bears deserved an invitation to the world championship tournament in Chicago. But we didn't get one. This was before the professional basketball association had a championship. The cosponsors of the world championship, the *Chicago Herald-Tribune* and the City of Chicago, usually invited the top winners of the various leagues. The Bears weren't part of any league, but we had beaten a lot of teams, and we were the only team in Washington, D.C. I thought the nation's capital ought to be represented.

So I decided to go to Chicago to see if I could personally wrangle an invitation to the four-day championship tournament. This was just one week before the tournament was scheduled to begin. The first person I contacted when I arrived in Chicago was Frank Forbes, who knew me as a sportswriter in

D.C. He had a radio show, and he invited me on to present my case, agreeing with me that the Bears belonged in the tournament. Frank also helped me get an appointment to see the mayor of Chicago, who knew that the response to Frank's radio show had been overwhelmingly in support of the Bears playing in the tournament. The mayor must have persuaded the tournament organizers, because the Bears finally got the invitation to play, although it came too late for us to be included in the printed program.

I immediately returned to Washington to contact the players, who had to get permission from their employers to take the time off from work. Then I had to make the travel arrangements. This was hard on short notice, but Abe Lichtman helped us out financially. Miraculously, I got all the guys on a train in New York the night before the first round of the tournament. We rode all night, arrived in Chicago around 10 A.M., and went straight to the stadium for the first game.

The tournament organizers were not too thrilled about having us shoved down their throats, and they thought they were going to get rid of us early by matching us against a White team from Sheboygan, Wisconsin, but we clobbered them. Advancing to the quarter finals, we faced the Rochester Royals, a National Basketball League squad. We had beaten them before, and we ran right through them, too.

By the time we reached the semifinals, we had caught the imagination of Chicago, just as we had Washington, D.C. We breezed through the semifinals, setting the stage for the final game against the Oshkosh All-Stars from Wisconsin. Twelve thousand fans jammed Chicago Stadium to see that match—

the biggest crowd in the arena's history, it was said. A lot was riding on that game.

A lot of gambling money was also riding on that game, and it seemed that some folks in Chicago stood to lose a lot if the Bears won. I was about to leave the hotel where we were staying and go to the stadium when the hotel clerk told me there were some people waiting to see me in the lobby. I didn't know who they could be, but I went down anyway, only to find that the four White men—very tall and very big, according to the clerk—had left. I put it out of my mind and left for the stadium.

I arrived in advance of the team and went down to check out the dressing rooms and make sure that everything was in order before the guys showed up. When I walked back out into the hall, four very large men suddenly surrounded me and hustled me through the crowded hallway to my dressing room. Once inside, they locked the door.

"We want to talk to you," one of them said. "You've got to lose this game tonight."

One of the other men reached inside a black traveling bag and pulled out a fistful of $100 bills. The rest of the bag was also full of hundreds.

"Money talks," he said. "You've got to lose this game."

"I don't know what you're talking about," I replied. "I can't control the ballplayers and I'm not gonna throw no games."

"I got $20,000 here to pay your players to lose. Money talks."

Obviously, this hood had a very limited vocabulary. But that was okay with me because my theme stayed the same too.

"No. I couldn't even approach the players with this kind of deal. It's impossible. Besides, I don't have anything to do with this team as far as the playing is concerned. Tarzan Cooper is the coach."

So they went to Tarzan, and Tarzan said, "You got the wrong man. You got the wrong people. We only play to win."

When they offered him the bag full of money, again he said, "No way."

Before they left, they came back to me and the thug holding the bag of money gave me one last warning.

"You be sure to lose that game if you want to get out of here," he said. "There's too much riding on this for us to lose."

If any of the players had been approached by the hoods, they didn't bring it up. I didn't either. I wanted them to concentrate on the game. When we gathered the team together for a pregame strategy meeting, we talked basketball, and basketball only. Our goal was to win.

But Tarzan had said to me, "I hope they don't do anything to us."

I said, "We're gonna take care of you."

There were a lot of Black hoods in Chicago, too, and I made some contacts. I was told, "Protect yourselves and be ready for a quick getaway."

So I quietly told the trainers and gofers to pack up and be ready. During the game, five chauffeur-driven black Cadillacs drove in under Chicago Stadium—our getaway cars.

Meanwhile the championship game was in progress, and it was close. Neither team ever established a comfortable lead, but we had a clear chance of winning. I had to inform the guys of what was going on so they would be ready to get out quick. I told them before the fourth quarter started, and I think the situation only made them more motivated. Tarzan was in top form that night, but it was Pops Gates, backed by Zack Clayton, who finally clinched it for the Bears by two points.

The Bears had swept the series and the crowd was on its feet roaring, but the new basketball world champions didn't even take a bow. We hurried off the court, and instead of going back to the dressing rooms, we headed through a side tunnel led by two Black hoods who had been sitting near our bench. These were some pretty tough guys, let me tell you—real roughnecks. I don't think they knew how to be afraid. The two hoods and the chauffeurs were all packing guns just in case anything went down.

Our luggage was already loaded into the cars and we piled in, too, the players still wearing their uniforms. The cars sped away from Chicago Stadium and then from the city itself. We ended up in Sheboygan, Wisconsin. The mobster who had arranged all this (a guy who owned two or three restaurants in Chicago) directed us to various private homes in Sheboygan, where we stayed the night. The next day, they took us to Oshkosh, where we boarded a train back to Washington. We never saw the guys who had threatened us, but we didn't feel safe until we were back in D.C.

We returned to a hero's welcome. The team members were due back at work, but they were given an extra day off so they could ride in a big parade down Pennsylvania Avenue to the White House. President Roosevelt, in a wheelchair, presented us with certificates of recognition, and there was a big dinner.

The famous sportswriter Grantland Rice knew how to capitalize on good publicity. As soon as the news of our win came over the wire, he started putting together a benefit game that would feature the Bears against an all-star team coached by Claire Bee, the White coach of the Long Island University Blackbirds. The proceeds would go to the Infantile Paralysis Fund, which of course is what the president suffered from. That benefit game was a landmark event. Grantland managed to get the Uline Arena, and for the first time a Black team played there. It was also the first time the audience was integrated. We raised about $60,000 for the fight against polio. It was a great homecoming.

The Washington Bears didn't last long after winning the 1943 championship title. It was getting too expensive to bring in the White pro teams, and the Black teams weren't in our class and didn't draw enough of a crowd. The payroll was phenomenal: the professionals demanded a whole lot of money.

Washington Bears, 1942

Also, the White teams were beginning to open up to Blacks: After the war was over, a lot of things started opening up. The basketball teams started integrating; so did the baseball teams. Sam Lacey was instrumental in bringing this about, and so was a guy named Wendell Smith from the *Pittsburgh Courier*. They put pressure on the team owners to give different Black ballplayers a try. Griffith, the owner of the stadium and of the Washington Senators, was one of the staunch hold-outs. I said to Griffith, "Why don't you take some of these Black ballplayers and put them on your team?" But his answer was, "Oh, no, no, you're not being reasonable. If you take all these good ballplayers and put them on the team, what are the Black ball teams gonna do?

"What we have is so plentiful," I said, "these ballplayers can be replaced in no time at all—if you would let these guys play." But it was like that with a lot of teams. George Preston Marshall, the owner of the Washington Redskins, didn't want any-

Baseball great Josh Gibson and Hal at exhibition game with proceeds going to the National Council of Negro Women.

body Black. He'd sell us all these expensive tickets, but we never got the
decent seating. The Yankees didn't
either.

Bill Veeck, owner of the Cleveland Indians, was one of the real pi-
oneers in integrating baseball. He
was the greatest, and he didn't
back up for one minute. Everybody else just gave lip service to
the idea. Bill Veeck brought
Satchel Paige to Cleveland. He
knew Satch wasn't the player he
used to be, but at least Bill gave
him a chance to play in the
major leagues. We were fighting so hard, and Griffith was
saying we were destroying
the Negro Leagues. Sam and
I explained that it was a matter of giving these ballplayers the opportunity to show what
they could do without being restricted by race.

Dolly King of the Washington Bears, a team owned by Hal, 1940s

As it turned out, the first Black player to break into White
basketball was our star Dolly King, who joined the Rochester
Royals. He was the first in a succession of extraordinary Black
players who would go on to change the face of professional
basketball into what we know it as today.

4.

THE HOUSE THAT JACK BUILT

uring the mid-1940s, you didn't have to purchase radio frequencies. If you found one that was available, you could apply for a license to program on it. A White newspaper publisher named Richard Eaton decided to branch out into the broadcasting business, so he investigated the frequencies and discovered that 1590 was available in the D.C. area. He then secured a license to broadcast on it, calling his new station WOOK.

Being a smart businessman, Eaton realized that there was a tremendous demand for Black-oriented programming, and he decided to aim for that market. I was the only Black announcer on the air in D.C. at the time, so he sent his attorney, Marv Willig, to talk to me about becoming a disc jockey on the new station. I was not hard to persuade. I wanted to be a full-time broadcaster, and at WOOK I'd get that chance.

The job I was offered was for Monday through Saturday, from the time the station went on the air until the time it went off at sundown. (In those days, many stations broadcast only during the daylight hours, and the length of the broadcast day varied with the time the sun set; sometimes you'd go off at 5 or 6 o'clock and, at other times, not until 9 o'clock.) I would have a three-hour lunch break, and during that time the station would have other programming, but I would be responsible for all the music. The contract they drew up for me called for a salary of $50 a week plus expenses. I had to sell all the advertising for my show, which was a common arrangement at the time, but I got a percentage of the revenue. I agreed to these terms because I would be a full-time, professional broad-

Hal's "Jackson's All Sports Club" in Washington, D.C., 1940s

caster—one of a handful of full-time professional Black broad-casters in the country. I also insisted that the contract allow me to keep my show on WINX, which was a late-night show. After finishing at WOOK, I went directly to WINX.

WOOK was located in a converted residence in Silver Springs, Maryland; it wasn't air-conditioned or soundproofed. The "studio" was a hot, airless, cramped space, but it was going to be my private domain for many hours every day. I took advantage of the magic of radio to create an imaginary house as the setting for my show, "The House That Jack Built." It was the era of "personality radio," and the most important thing a successful host did was to create a personality and the setting to go with it. In my imagination—and in that of my listeners—it was a large, comfortable home with a spacious living room and a terrace, an upstairs and a downstairs. I'd open the show with, "How are you? This is Hal Jackson, the host that loves you most, welcoming you to *The House That Jack Built*. We're rolling out the musical carpet, and we'll be spinning a few just for you. So come on in and sit back, relax, and enjoy your favorite recording stars from here to Mars."

I chose all the records myself, although Richard Eaton made it clear that I was to stick to those by Black artists—"race music," as it was called then. I played Nat Cole and Dinah Washington and the Ink Spots because they were great artists, and once in a while I would slip in a record by Peggy Lee or some other White performer whose work I liked. To me, it was the quality of the music, not the color of the performer, that mattered. As I introduced each record, I pretended I was wandering around my imaginary house and coming across the various artists in the living room or on the terrace. I'd say, "Let's go out on the terrace now. Oh boy, look who's sitting there—four guys out of Baltimore! They are called the Orioles. Let me tell you a little about the Orioles. Sonny Til is the leader of the group. He got this group together when the guys were still in high school. They used to rehearse outside the school, on the doorsteps and on street corners, and little by little they learned to blend their harmony together. Everybody, not only in Baltimore but all over the country, learned to love this group. Here now are the Orioles singing their big hit, 'What Is There to Say.'"

Sometimes my introduction was longer than the record. We played 78s in those days, and they were really short.

The audience really got involved in this imaginary world. They would write in and say, "Hal, when you go out on the terrace today, wish me a happy birthday. My family and I will be sitting out there on our terrace waiting." I would honor those requests, and mention a lot of listeners' names on the show, because that was a great audience builder.

When I signed off, I'd say, "I've gotta pack the shellac and hit the track, but I'll be back."

The show really caught on, and soon I was able to attract recognized performers to the studio for interviews on the air. It wasn't easy considering conditions in the "studio" and the fact that they had to make a long trip out to suburban Maryland. That place was like an oven in the summer, and our air-conditioning system was a fan sitting on a block of ice. When interviewing artists on really hot days, I kept the fan close so they weren't too uncomfortable. One day I reached over to put a record on the turntable, and the fan caught my thumb and split it wide open. Blood was spurting out everywhere—but I was the only disc jockey, and if I had gone to the hospital, they would have had to close down the station. The manager pleaded, "Don't go! Don't go!" so I stayed. The manager called a doctor to come down to the station, and he sewed the cut up while I continued broadcasting.

I was the key to the whole enterprise. I did all the news. Most news broadcasters in those days could at least "rip and read," which meant tearing the Associated Press and United Press International wire service reports off the ticker machine and reading them. But WOOK didn't have a news ticker, so I prepared my news reports by scanning the morning and afternoon papers and ad-libbing the main stories when it was time to do the news. I did the same thing for sports reports, which were easy to embellish because of my interest in sports and because I was still writing for the *Afro-American.*

I also did all the commercials. I didn't just create the spots, I went out and solicited the advertisers. The commercials were my main source of income, so I spent much of my time off the air recruiting sponsors. I had to do this mostly by telephone, because WOOK was not exactly in the Black community. In fact, except for the maids and other domestic help, I was probably the only Black person going regularly to Silver Springs. And during the summer, when the station didn't go off the air until as late as 9 P.M., I know I was the only Black person on the streets at night.

Richard Eaton was concerned about that. Fearing that the community, which was pretty bigoted, would object if they

Hal with Joe "The Brown Bomber" Louis
and his manager, 1940s

saw me or realized that a radio station aimed at Black Washington was in their midst, he wanted me to keep a low profile. But he proved to be wrong, and keeping a low profile has never been one of my strong suits. My show was me, and from the letters and telephone calls I was getting, I knew that I had a lot of listeners in Silver Springs—especially among the young people. After I started the Good Deed Club, there was no hope of me remaining anonymous.

One of my mottoes has always been "It's nice to be important, but it's important to be nice," and that was the philosophy of the Good Deed Club. I think it started after someone called me at the station and told me that there was a lady in the hospital who wanted to listen to *The House That Jack Built* but couldn't because she didn't have a radio. I mentioned this on the air, and the response was astounding. People called in with offers to donate a radio to the lady. Then hospitals started calling to say they also had patients who needed radios. Radio repair shops called to offer to fix broken radios free of charge, and cab companies offered to take the radios to hospitals. Within a week or two, we had brought in, repaired, and delivered about 300 radios to local hospitals. I was very gratified by the response.

The Good Deed Club really caught on. Club members volunteered in hospitals and convalescent homes. They repaired broken toys and donated them to the children's wards in hospitals. We collected more than 15,000 books and magazines and distributed them to fourteen hospitals from Richmond to Baltimore. I was invited to make appearances at the suburban White schools, getting the youngsters together to volunteer their services as part of the Good Deed Club. The club also sponsored benefit shows, whose proceeds went to charitable causes.

Although I was accepted—even honored—by much of the Silver Springs community, I was too far from my primary audience to be able to help them in the way that I wanted, or to build up the sponsorship of my show. I was getting a lot of invitations to do personal appearances in Washington's Black community, but being so far away made it impossible for me to accept many of them. Richard Eaton realized that we needed

Sergeant Joe Louis with Mrs. Sidat-Singh and Hal after the tragic death of Sidat-Singh (Washington Bears and Syracuse University Varsity player) during pilot flight training, 1944

to move if we were going to increase the station's visibility, so we looked around for rental space in Washington and eventually found a place on Connecticut Avenue at K Street, an area that was traditionally all White. But I had no trouble there, and it made life a lot easier, if no less hectic.

Sponsorship of my show really started to build after we moved to Washington. I now had the opportunity to visit more sponsors to attract advertising. I spent a lot of my off-air time generating new business and a lot of my on-air time doing commercials. I learned how to bunch them into groups of three or four, and I could get as many as twenty 60-second commercials into an hour. I did a lot of commercials in rhyme, just as I did in my show *The House That Jack Built*. I've always been good at that, and the audience liked it. I would interweave my rhymes with bits of music from records and bring up the music while I was talking, so listeners would think they were listening to music when they were really getting a commercial message.

I also did a lot of remotes—broadcasting from a store or restaurant or car dealership. Not only did this give variety to the show, it also brought customers to the sponsor. The store or business would advertise that Hal Jackson would be there on Saturday, and people would come to see me and get my autograph. Auto Wholesalers, a car dealership in Washington, was one of my biggest local sponsors. I would do remotes from the lot. I would turn on the engine of a car and say to my listeners, "Look, I'm sitting in a 1946 Chevrolet, and I want you to come out to Auto Wholesalers and let me show it to you." Pretty soon, a dozen or more cars would be pulling into the lot. It was amazing how many cars we sold as a result of those remotes.

Once we started broadcasting from Washington, I was able to attract national sponsors, among them National Beer. In addition to the on-air advertising, I would do special promotions for them, such as appearing at a local club that agreed to serve nothing but National Beer while I was there.

I should mention at this point that I took my responsibility as a spokesman for all these products seriously. I never ac-

Hal during **WLIB** *Christmas fund-raisers for children, 1950s*

cepted a sponsorship without first checking out the sponsor
and the product. I made sure that the merchandise advertised
was actually available and at the advertised price, that there
were no bait-and-switch schemes going on. I turned down
commercials that were in questionable taste, and I refused to
advertise products that I thought were demeaning to Blacks,

like hair straighteners and bleaching creams. This caused no end of arguments with Richard Eaton, whose eye was always on the bottom line. I stood firm, because I believed that my most important asset as a communicator was trust, and I wasn't about to violate it.

There was nothing wrong with cigarette advertising in those days, and one of my national sponsors was Philip Morris. At one point they were interested in sponsoring my football broadcasts from Howard University and asked about my ratings. Well, Howard University wasn't hooked into Hooper, which was the rating service at that time, so I just took the Philip Morris people out to the Black community and stopped people on the street and asked them who they listened to on the radio. In 7 cases out of 10, the answer was "Hal Jackson." That convinced them.

In many cases, I signed personal contracts with sponsors, meaning that they would follow me wherever I went, even to a competing station. That gave me a lot of leverage with Richard Eaton, and I was able to do pretty much what I wanted.

One day, Morris Blum, who owned station WANN in Annapolis, Maryland, approached me about doing a show. He had recognized the great potential of the Black audience, and he wanted someone the audience was familiar with. Eaton was not thrilled about lending me to a potential competitor, but I had so many personal sponsors he really couldn't do much about it.

I wanted to be fair to Eaton, so I made him an offer that had something in it for him. By this time Eaton had picked up another station—WSID in Essex, outside of Baltimore, Maryland—and I told him I would do an afternoon sports report on WSID if he would let me do the WANN show. Eaton decided that I should have more exposure on WSID and finally agreed to the arrangement if I would do a five-hour show for him on that station. Shortly afterward, I began what was probably the most hectic work period of my entire life.

I would wake up in the morning at about 4:30 and drive over to Connecticut Avenue and K Street to do the 6 o'clock wake-up show on WOOK. At midday, I would drive out to Annapolis, 30 miles away, and do a two-hour show over WANN. Then I'd get back into the car and drive to Essex and do five hours over WSID. Finally, I would drive back to Washington for

Hal with Duke Ellington and Duke's manager at Sparrow's Beach, Maryland, late 1940s

my show over WINX, which by this time had expanded to a
three-hour show, from 10 P.M. to 1 A.M. As I was driving from
one station to another, I would mentally shift to the new station, and I don't believe I ever got the call letters mixed up.
One smart thing I did was to keep the show's name the same.
It was *The House That Jack Built* no matter what station I was
on. When I was getting ready to sign off, I'd tell my listeners
that I was taking the House on the road. The show's offerings
did vary from station to station, however. Country and western
music was big around Annapolis, so I included more of that
kind of music when I was broadcasting over WANN. Unlike
Richard Eaton, Morris Blum didn't insist that I stick to race
music. Since Eaton wanted me to focus on sports on WSID, I
included a lot of sports reporting on my show out of Essex,
Maryland.

Not only was I all over the dial, I was also all over the region, doing benefits and making personal appearances. In addition to the remotes from sponsors' places of business that I
kept doing because it was good business to do so, I was in con-
stant demand to emcee at benefit fund-raisers for various worthy causes. And I used my position as a celebrity in the region
to identify and help out my own worthy causes.

Oscar Haynes featured me in one of his "Around the Dial"
columns in the *Washington Herald* around that time. It gives a
good idea of what my life was like in those days, and I'll quote
from it:

> *So you want to be a disc jockey, huh?*
> *This column is not intended to discourage you, but*

rather a reminder that his life, "a disc jockey's," is not peaches and cream.

The busiest person in Washington is one of the city's most popular disc jockeys—Harold Jackson, emcee of "The House that Jack Built," WINX. His schedule of "routine" activities for one week would make the date book of a popular sub-deb look like a clean sheet of paper.

With the exception of his full-time radio job, practically all of Harold's activities are for a charitable or civic cause, for which he receives no pay. This may not seem important, but to be a popular disc jockey with a good Hooper rating, you must be well known and active in the community. This has been the secret of this record spinner's success.

The public is always demanding the services of a top-flight disc jockey and if he is to maintain his popularity he never says no. In one week, Harold made 16 guest-appearances for clubs, civic organizations, and benefit performances. Meanwhile, he was compelled to keep up routine visits to several veterans' and children's hospitals, old folks' homes and other institutions.

Besides the routine visits, he was busy obtaining magazines, books and radios for distribution to hospitals. . . .

Meanwhile, the popular disc jockey has his full-time radio job. In most instances he has a morning or early-afternoon program and another evening program that runs into the early A.M. hours. Before going on the air, he must select his records, prepare his script and check his operations schedule.

While the rest of the city is playing, he is working. This includes holidays when everyone wants to be free from his job to go and do what he wishes.

Do you still want to be a disc jockey? It takes much perseverance.

Although Haynes was right that I needed to do charity work to maintain my popularity, I did more than was necessary because I enjoyed doing good deeds. I started Christmas drives for needy people. The first year, my goal was to collect toys, food, and clothing for 200 families whose names I got from local churches. I arranged for my listeners to drop off donations at various locations, and I did remotes from those locations, interviewing people when they brought their donations in. This was a big hit, and we collected enough gifts to distribute to about 6,000 families that Christmas.

The situation was bad for poor, Black unwed mothers in those days. Well-to-do girls could take a "vacation" and have their babies somewhere else. But if you were poor and Black, and your family couldn't or didn't want to help you, you were in trouble. So I helped raise funds for a home for these girls in Anacostia, in southeast Washington, so they had a place to stay during their pregnancy and could give birth under proper conditions. I also helped raise more funds so they could have counseling and job training and support themselves and their babies after they left the home. I even managed to find jobs for some of them.

Meanwhile, my own three children were growing up so rapidly I could scarcely believe it. You may be wondering how

I found the time to be home. Well, I didn't spend much time there. I was too busy trying to make a living so I could support my family. But the truth is, I didn't feel very welcome in my own house. My mother-in-law was a wedge between Julia and me, and I think that some of my efforts out in the community were a way of seeking the appreciation that I didn't feel I got at home.

5.

NEW WORLDS TO CONQUER

y the late 1940s, Black people in the United States were beginning to push for change. World War II had a lot to do with the new sense of entitlement. After all, thousands of Black men had served their country in the military, making the world safe for democracy, only to return home and find the same old segregation waiting for them. Roosevelt and Truman had given us hope; Roosevelt's New Deal social programs helped matters at home, and Truman had issued an executive order banning discrimination in the military.

Meanwhile, at Howard University, Charles Hastie had succeeded in turning the Law School into the "West Point of the South." Attorneys he trained were using the nation's basic laws to secure equitable salaries for teachers and to fight "separate-but-equal" education. I was too busy to continue my course work at Howard by that time, but I remained close to the school through my broadcasts of its athletic contests, and I kept up with what was going on. Most of the attorneys and law students were active in the Washington branch of the NAACP, and since I was a strong advocate of breaking down racial barriers, it was natural that some of my fund-raising work would be on its behalf.

For three years, I handled the fund-raising for the capital branch of the NAACP, with every penny I raised going to the organization. The most successful event I organized was a benefit marathon that took place in all the cities where I was doing radio shows. I put together a group of artists and musicians and took them to Annapolis, where we did a two-hour benefit in one of the city's large auditoriums. Then we drove to Baltimore to broadcast the same show live from the Met Theater before an audience of 3,000. We then returned to Washington, where even more artists joined us, and put on a midnight show at the Howard Theater. I don't remember how much money we raised, but it was substantial. The work involved was killing—especially on top of my already exhausting schedule. Lining up the artists and the venues, doing all the advance publicity necessary to make the event a success, and then hosting back-to-back shows was too much even for me. When that marathon was over, I collapsed and had to be hospitalized for exhaustion.

I did more than fund-raising for the NAACP; I had its executive director, Walter White, on my radio shows. (I also had Whitney Young of the National Urban League, and Congressman Adam Clayton Powell Jr. on at various times to talk about the struggle for equality.) I organized protests, among them picket lines in front of some of the stores on Connecticut Avenue that would sell merchandise to Black customers but wouldn't let them use the dressing rooms or restrooms. I got involved in demonstrations demanding that Negroes be trained and hired for jobs downtown.

Richard Eaton, the owner of two of the stations that broadcast *The House that Jack Built*, was not happy about my political activism. He didn't mind Christmas drives for the needy, but fund-raising and organizing protests for the NAACP were another matter. He told me straight out that I could not be involved in controversial issues and remain on the air. I answered, "Look, when I'm off the air, I can use my time as I wish, and I will not let you interfere with my fighting for the rights of Black people." I was too valuable for him to make good on his threat, and he let me go my own way—until I started trying to organize a union at WOOK.

My working conditions were as good as could be expected at a station the size of WOOK, and I was making a decent living—not from the salary Eaton paid me but from my percentages of advertising revenues. Nevertheless I was still one of the few Blacks in radio in the D.C. area. I had managed to bring in some other Blacks, at various levels, but I wanted more, and I wanted them to be paid a decent wage.

When I tried to pressure Eaton to improve salaries and working conditions for others at the station, he couldn't understand why I bothered, since I was doing okay. My protest work with the NAACP had made me more aware of labor unions and the good they could do in bettering conditions for workers. So I joined the American Federation of Radio Artists (AFRA, which later added television people and became AFTRA) and got AFRA to start organizing the people at WOOK. When Eaton refused the union's demands, we called a strike. Eaton refused to back down and

Hal and Louis Jordan during Hal's live television show from the Howard Theater Dumont network, 1949

brought in strikebreakers to keep the station on the air. Some Blacks crossed the picket lines, and that hurt me a little, but I understood that they wanted to get on the radio so badly that they would do anything. WOOK lost a lot of revenue during the strike, and Eaton eventually had to give in and allow the union, but by that time there was so much bad feeling between the two of us that I did not feel I could return. That was the end of my association with WOOK.

It was 1949, and, fortunately for me, a lot of things were changing. One day I got a call from the advertising agency that had gotten me started in radio, Cal Ehrlich and Merrick, asking me if I wanted to take *The House That Jack Built* to television.

Television was a brand–new medium then. It had first been introduced to the public at the 1939 World's Fair in New York City. Washington, D.C., had four stations—three network stations and one independent, WTTG, Channel 5, owned by Dumont, which also owned an outlet in New York. There were very few television sets in private homes, especially Black homes, so it seemed to me premature to try to reach Blacks through television. In 1948, the Black singer and pianist Bob Howard had a series called *Sing It Again*, but it was soon canceled for lack of sponsorship. But Emerson, which made radios, and now televisions, and had been one of my big sponsors on radio for some time, wanted to sponsor a weekly television variety show aimed at the minority market, and they wanted me to do it. So unlike Bob Howard, who couldn't get a sponsor, I had a sponsor coming to me.

The only variety shows on television were out of New York. Ed Sullivan's was the best known. Arthur Godfrey also had one. Godfrey had a radio show out of Washington, D.C., but he commuted up to New York to do his television show. I liked the idea of hosting the first television variety show out of Washington, and I especially liked the idea of featuring Black performers, since we were conspicuously absent from the White variety shows. The only exception was the *Lucky Strike Hit Parade*, where Frank Sinatra shocked everyone by featuring artists like the Mills Brothers and Nat Cole, who even had his own show for a while in the mid-1950s. But Frank Sinatra was in a class by himself.

My imagination went to work, and I came up with the idea of broadcasting the show from the Howard Theater instead of from a studio. This was before Ed Sullivan moved his show to Broadway. I persuaded the Emerson people to agree to this by pointing out that they could sell more product, since they would have a theater full of people as well as the television audience to pitch their products to.

The show debuted in the spring of 1949, on Monday nights from 7:30 to 8:30. The work involved was not much different from radio. I produced the show, booked the performers, wrote the script, most of which I ad-libbed, and did all the commercials using props provided by Emerson. It was all live, no retakes, so if I made a mistake I just had to collect myself and go on; but I was a pro by this time, and I didn't make many mistakes.

For my first show, I had Stan Kenton and his big band as guests. During the year or so the show was on the air I had just about every top performer of the day: Duke Ellington and his orchestra were on one show; Al Hibler and Ray Nance were featured soloists, and Kay Davis was the vocalist. Johnny Hartman, Sarah Vaughan, and Billy Eckstein all appeared on the show as well. Woody Herman and his Herd were on one show, the Mills Brothers on another. Louie Jordan and his orchestra were on at the time they had their big hit, "Run Joe," and Sammy Davis Jr. was with the group. Louie was worried about putting Sammy on the air for fear that another band leader would discover how good he was and try to steal him away. As a matter of fact, I don't think Sammy stayed with Louie for long after that. Another singer who got her first big television break on my show was Dinah Washington.

In addition to nationally known performers, I showcased a lot of local talent. Singer Ruth Brown and band leader Tiny Bradshaw were two of the local artists who got their first exposure on my show.

I stayed on the radio, which I still considered my main forum, arranging for coverage on Monday nights so I could do the television show. The medium was opening up more to Blacks by that time, and I started getting offers from small stations in New York. Then, as now, New York was considered the big time: you really hadn't made it unless you had made it in New York. Billie Rowe and Major Robinson, two columnists

☆ *Hal and D.J. Coral in Washington, D.C., 1940*

Harold Jackson
Returning to D.C.

NEW YORK — Harold Jackson, radio and television star, who has taken Washington, Baltimore, and New York by storm announced to the New York Press Club over the week end that he was returning to Washington.

The reason, the Mutual Broadcasting System outlet in Washington, WEAM, has turned over five hours of broadcasting to his "House That Jack Built" program.

Jackson who was the first sepia radio and TV star in the nation's capital said that "Things were getting ready in Washington to go all out to give all citizens in the nation's capital the right to live as first class citizens and I want to be on hand to do all that I can to aid in the fight.

"New York has been wonderful to me and all of the press has been too, but I feel that being on a network station and co-operating with all of our organization I can help to aid my people in gaining something that they should have had years ago."

HAL JACKSON
RETURNS TO WASHINGTON
•
ENJOY AUTO WHOLESALER'S
'HOUSE THAT JACK BUILT'
•
STARTING APRIL 10
MONDAY THRU THURSDAY
•
6–7 A. M. ★ 11 P. M.–1 A. M.
WEAM ⟶ 1390
MUTUAL IN WASHINGTON

☆ *Clippings announcing Hal's Movietone Show, 1940s*

HAL JACKSON MOVIETONE SHOW—A brand-new radio show at Club Twenty-Eleven opened last week with Hal Jackson, disc jockey at WEAM, and his Movietone Show. Guests and representatives of the Movietone Television Corporation are having quite a time in celebrating their newest innovation for meeting the public's demand for genuine entertainment. In the picture can be seen: (seated) Irving Nigoro, Geraldine Howie, Edgar Anderson, Richard Fortune, Clyde Lee, Sol Slade. Mrs. Slade, Harry Becker, Jack Seibloth. Edward Sweet, Phil Nigoro, Louis Taff, Paul Schneider. (Standing) Harold Jackson, Harry Goldberg, Bernie Taff and Walter Hirsch.

AUTO WHOLESALERS'
HAL JACKSON
TWO SHOWS DAILY!
6:00 TO 7:45 **A.M.** | 11:00 TO 11:55 **P.M.**
WEAM • 1390
MUTUAL IN WASHINGTON

☆ WLIB *promotional poster, 1950s*

☆ *Hal Jackson promoting Budweiser for*
WWRL, *late 1950s*

Dear Mr. Retailer:

COCA-COLA is on the air . . . with a bigger advertising schedule than ever on Hal Jackson's popular "House that Jack Built" every day on WLIB.

So be sure to stock up on plenty of delicious, refreshing COCA-COLA . . . both in regular size and big, BIG, Family Size . . . and keep well displayed. Because a lot of WLIB listeners will be coming into your store to buy.

WLIB
Harlem's Radio Center
2090 Seventh Avenue   •   New York 27
1190 ON THE DIAL

☆ WLIB *Coca-Cola promotions, 1950s*

☆ *Hal and Milton Berle, 1950s*

☆ Hal receiving Disc Jockey of the Year award from Richard Chamberland, 1960s

☆ The Reverend David Licorice preaching in protest to unwarranted bribery charges against Hal in the payola scandal, early 1960s

☆ Hal Jackson outside courthouse with attorney Earl Warren Zaidins, after being cleared from payola scandal, early 1960s

WE JUST WANTED TO SAY . . .

". . . dedication and respect for his fellow man personify Hal Jackson. It has been men like Hal who have helped make this country great."

Ed Brooke
U. S. Senator

•

"Having had the pleasure of knowing Hal since his early broadcasting days in Washington, D.C., I am honored to join in his many friends in thanking him for a job well done."

Walter Washington
Mayor, Washington, D.C.

•

"Hal Jackson is a man who has reached out and touched many hands . . ."

Diana Ross

•

"Hal Jackson is a spiritual being . . ."

Stevie Wonder

•

". . . sorry I could not be there, but continued best wishes."

Telly Savalas

•

"It gives me great pleasure to join in the salute to Hal Jackson, who has contributed immeasurably to all New Yorkers—Young and old."

Robert F. Wagner, Sr.
Former Ambassador and Mayor

"Right on Hal! Keep on truckin' . . ."

Sammy Davis, Jr.

•

"On a joyous night, I would like to add a serious note: Thank you for your many efforts on behalf of those who need our help so much."

Jerry Lewis

•

"Thank you for being there . . ." **Peggy Lee**

•

"Hal Jackson started off on the "good foot" and has never looked back."

James Brown

•

"If you ever stop helping people, Hal Jackson, I'm gonna bust you upside your head."

Redd Foxx

•

"Peace, Love and soul . . ." **Don Cornelius**

•

"We all say thank you Hal." **Ellis Haitlip**

"The devil didn't make me do this—Best wishes, Hal."

Flip Wilson

•

"The Pips and I join in expressing our gratitude for your friendship over the years."

Gladys Knight

Right on Hal
Loving's

Aretha Franklin

"Best of luck in your future endeavors."

Earl Monroe

•

"Hal Jackson, is one heck of a beautiful person. A warm guy who has helped a lot of people get started: including Percy Sutton."

Percy Sutton
Borough President, Manhattan

•

"Hal Jackson should be commended for his unselfish efforts to bring to the attention of countless thousands the importance of being Black . . ."

Eddie O'Jay

"It's nice to be important, but it's important to be nice."

The Osmond Family

•

"I'm so very appreciative of the fact that Hal Jackson continues to give me credit for bringing him to New York. Because of his enormous success this makes me look so good that I must now tell the truth . . . I was paid to get him out of Washington."

Billy Rowe

•

"I first met Hal Jackson over 20 years ago. Ageless Hal, is the same wonderful guy today that he was then. Perhaps his secret is that he is unaffected by adversity or success and treats those two imposters just the same."

David Dinkins

•

"HAL JACKSON has a deep understanding of human needs. The world is improved because Hal Jackson is part of it. I call him 'Mr. Warm, Sincere and Wonderful.'"

Joe Franklin

•

"If it wasn't for guys like Hal Jackson, guys like me wouldn't be."

Al Gee

☆ Hal with the Labor Panel of the nationally televised Cerebral Palsy Telethon, 1970s

☆ Hal Jackson and Stevie Wonder strategizing their Save the Children of Atlanta effort, 1970s

☆ Hal Jackson with Ahmet Ertegun, 1970s

☆ *Marvin Gaye and Hal, 1970s*

☆ *Charity work with the Cerebral Palsy Telethon, 1971*

Helping hand

SICKLE CELL ANEMIA victim Vivian Givens, age 9, shown sitting on lap of disc jockey Hal Jackson (top center), seems very much like all the other dance students at the Bob Fournier-Hal Grego Dance Academy. Some time ago she began to show signs of extreme weakness and fatigue, but refused to complain to her teachers and parents. Finally it became apparent that Vivian needed medical attention. The crushing blow came unexpectedly. Sickle Cell Anemia had found another victim. Like many people Fournier and Grego, directors of the Academy, had never heard of the dreaded disease. When they learned more about it, they decided to act, and with the help of Hal Jackson a march to collect money to help the fight against the disease was staged in Brooklyn. They did more than march. On Sept. 12 on Channel 9 it was announced during the Sickle Cell Anemia Telethon that the Fournier-Grego Dance Academy students collected and donated $5,000 in honor of all the Vivian Givens of the world. Fournier is shown standing in back row, and Grego, (1st., left). Others in photo taken at Palisades Amusement Park are: Dayle Carpenter (on Jackson's right), Vinnie Dee and Leslie Dockery (left), Louisa Harris (sitting, right) and other fund raisers not identified.

☆ *Melba Moore and Hal, 1970s*

oon then went
lapse, affecting
.. Today, there
st movement in
ngland herself
to get out of
'e Gods, even
tist movement.
rfectly obvious
he dominoes is
ollpase of the
which they were
tails of kites,
with their

States is now
turing its own
why the little

tish empire, the
ried in the Far
China has been
mminent fall of
'ambodia. The
rma, Indonesia
ext.
dy, the Israeli
put under dual
the Arab states

...d Norwegian

Hal Jackson To Be Honored Fri.

On Friday in the grand
ballroom of the New York Hilton
Hotel the radio and music
industry, unions, corporations
and countless individuals will
gather in support of one unique
man -- a tribue to Hal Jackson,
"the house that Jack built."

The famed raio personality,
known as the first full time black
announcer in the country and
pioneer throughout the industry
in general, has worked diligently
for over 25 years toward making
strides within the industry and in
lending his talents and efforts to
countless charitable causes.

The proceeds of this dinner will
all go to the Hal Jackson
Scholarship Foundation with a
special scholarship to Howard
University's department of
communications.

HAL JACKSON

St. Cr
Chanc
'Charli

FREDERIK
the CVI theat
Croix of "Y(
Charlie Brow
and may be ;
bookstore an(
office in Chri
in Sunny Isle
La Reine, Tr
Frederiksted,
from memb
players.
The visitin
seen for o
Saturday Ap
Center in Fre
is $2 for
children.___
Admit yo'
save many u:

TODAY'S CROSSWORD

 DAILY NEWS *tribute clip,* 1975

 Hal Jackson receiving
NAACP's *Image Award,*
1976

☆ *Cab Calloway and Hal, 1980s*

☆ *Hal and Ella Fitzgerald, 1980s*

★ *Mick Jagger and Hal, 1980s*

★ *Hal and members of Sister Sledge at
Radio City Music Hall, 1982*

☆ Janet Jackson and Hal at welcoming luncheon for the Hal Jackson's Talented Teen International contest, 1985

☆ Joey Morant and Senator Hollings greet Hal as he returns to his place of birth in Charleston, South Carolina, 1987

★ *Hal and Spike Lee promoting*

DO THE RIGHT THING, *1989*

★ *Hal and Nancy Wilson at*
Congressional Black Caucus, 1989

⭐ *Gregory Hines and Hal (Hines was one of Hal's childhood discoveries), late 1980s*

⭐ *The Temptations, Vaughn Harper, and Hal in Atlantic City, late 1980s*

*Susan L. Taylor, editor-in-chief of ESSENCE magazine,
with Hal, late 1980s*

*BOYZ II MEN at Hal Jackson's Talented Teens
International contest, 1991*

El De Barge, Mike Tyson, Hal, Vaughn Harper, and Heavy D during Hal Jackson's Talented Teens International contest, 1991

Wynton Marsalis and Hal at 21 Club reception celebrating jazz, early 1990s

Advertisement for WINX *broadcasting play–by–play of Howard University football, 1949*

for New York's Black weekly, *The Amsterdam News*, were among the most persuasive. They kept telling me that it was time to move on up.

Through my involvement with AFRA (American Federation of Radio Artists) I had gotten to know Morris Novick, who controlled a national daily show sponsored by the union on the ABC radio network. He and his brother, Harry, wanted to buy WLIB, which was owned at that time by the *New York Post*. The Brooklyn-based station operated only in the daytime with a very weak signal, and it featured foreign-language programming— Polish, Yiddish, Italian. The Novicks wanted to change the programming to English, concentrate on music, move it to Harlem,

Hal with Nat King Cole and Billy Rowe
of the PITTSBURGH COURIER, *1951*

and aim it at the Black market. To do that, they needed a name Black announcer.

There were many more Black announcers to choose from in the New York area. Willie Bryant had a late-night show from the Baby Grand on 125th Street on a station that broadcast in Italian in the daytime but switched to Black programming at night. Bill Cooke did *Cookie's Caravan* out of Newark but beamed at Harlem. But the Novicks wanted someone who could help them turn the station around, and they wanted me.

I had reservations about going to the Big Apple. I remembered the few months I had spent there when I was 15; I hadn't found it a very welcoming place. It was so big, so easy for a young kid to get lost there. But things were different now. I was a celebrity in Washington, and I knew people in New York. It was a new world to conquer, and if the challenges I faced were different—I wouldn't have to practically invent Black radio in New York—they were still challenges.

There was a lot of programming aimed at the Black audience in New York. In addition to the Black personalities I have mentioned, there were some strong White disc jockeys. The king of Black music in New York City was Symphony Sid, a Jewish guy who broadcast a morning and evening show over WWRL out of Woodside, Queens. And there was Freddy Robbins, who did a show aimed at Blacks, *Robbins' Nest*, from the Royal Roost, a nightclub on Broadway. His station was also foreign language in the daytime and English at night. Freddy featured a lot of celebrity interviews. William B. Williams was on the same station as Freddy, in an earlier time slot—not yet the big celebrity he would later become, but already proving that he was a radio personality to be reckoned with. There were only so many sponsors interested in

WASHINGTON POST *article about*

Hal Jackson's new position at

WUST, *1952*

WUST Rolls On *WASH POST*
3/1/52

Name Change Saves
Small Radio Station

——*By George T. Draper*——

A SMALL radio station that balanced on the brink of financial disaster in Bethesda has been saved by changing its name, moving to U st. and plugging hot jazz, blues and Negro spirituals.

Two other ingredients in the successful comeback of WUST, which formerly used the call letters WBCC, are Harold E. Sheffers, the general manager, and Harold Jackson, a Negro disc jockey with a large Atlantic Coast following.

Last Tuesday, WUST celebrated the fourth month of its comeback by moving into new, ultra-modern offices at 1343 U st. nw.

Jackson

It had been broadcasting its new line of music since leaving Bethesda in October from the lobby of the Republic Theater next door.

"WE HAD a well thought out plan," Sheffers said yesterday. "This was going to be an entirely different operation from the old WBCC.

"We decided to beam directly to that class of people who like this type of music . . . I'd call it music in a blues vein mixed with hot jazz."

Sheffers said favorites on his programs are the smokey blues of Ella Fitzgerald, the lively ballads of Rosemary Clooney, the plaintive melodies of the King Cole Trio and Les Brown's smooth symphonic jazz.

In the morning hours, WUST is likely to broadcast Negro spirituals with commentary by Frances White, a spiritualist disk jockey.

WITH THIS SORT of programing, Sheffers is now able to sit back and proudly proclaim that "we're running in the black" for the first time since 1946, when WBCC first went on the air in Bethesda.

Harold Jackson moved over to WUST from the new WOL and has built up a large following with his Monday-through-Friday "Sports Page" from 1 p. m. to 5 p. m. The program is a mixture of disc jockey commentary, hot music, sports news and horserace results.

Although the management of the station changed when Sheffers took over in October, after giving up his job as sales manager for WTTG—Dumont TV—the ownership has remained the same.

THE BIG SHARE of WUST is owned by Harold S. Russell, a Chicago businessman and owner of a railway supply and paint business. Other owners include W. Parker Jones and Carl J. Batter, both Washington lawyers.

No one could be more pleased with the success of the rejuvenated station than Batter, who frankly admits he was beginning to take a dim view of pumping money into the project.

"For some reason, we just couldn't make a go of it in Bethesda," he said, "and we had to take a chance on a new type of operation in Washington. It's beginning to look like the chance we took was right."

Hal's children: Jane, Jewell, and Hal Junior, 1947

reaching the African-American market, and I was aware that the competition would be fierce.

There were other reasons to stay in Washington. My family didn't want to move—my daughters were in school, and we didn't want to uproot them—so going to New York would mean having to maintain two households. The salary the Novicks offered me—I think it was $300 a week—was really not enough to make the move financially worthwhile, especially considering all the percentages from advertising I was giving up. I would have to do a lot of commuting and see my family even less than usual. But I was ready for something new, so after the Novicks succeeding in buying WLIB from the *Post* for $85,000, I accepted the offer to become their number one announcer, signing a one-year contract with an option to renew. The contract called for me to do a morning show from 7:15 to 10 A.M., and then return to the air from 3 P.M. until the station went off the air at sunset to make room for a station out of Fort Wayne, Indiana. The Novicks had moved the studio to 30th Street in midtown Manhattan, in the same building that housed the studios of Columbia Records, and they put me up at the nearby Hotel New Yorker. But I broadcast as often as I could from Harlem, where the audience I wanted to attract was located.

The *House That Jack Built* debuted on WLIB in 1949 at the station on West 30th Street. A couple of months later, we moved to our new permanent location in the Skyline Ballroom of the Hotel Theresa in Harlem. The manager of the hotel was the father of Ron Brown, the late secretary of commerce who died so tragically and so young in that air crash in Croatia in 1996. Ron was just a kid at the time, but he was already a star. That same year, he appeared in the first Pepsi advertisement aimed at Black consumers. The ad shows a little boy, Ron, reaching up to the six-pack of Pepsi his mother is holding high in the air. He was also displaying the entrepreneurship that would later make him such a successful businessman. He would run around the hotel getting autographs from Jackie Robinson, Joe Louis, Lena Horne—all the big stars stayed at the Theresa—and then he would sell those autographs to the neighborhood kids. I gave him his first job, running errands and helping me put records on the turntable.

I called the debut show a "Salute to Harlem," and featured a lot of celebrity guest stars. The headline in one of the local Black papers that week read "New Disk Jock Hits Like Avalanche in Harlem, NYC." In reality, a lot of my intended audience had trouble picking up the station's signal, it was so weak and there was a lot of interference from the tall buildings in midtown Manhattan. After a few months, the studio was moved out to Long Island, from which it was easier to beam the signal into Harlem.

I spent the first few months trying to establish the show in its primary market. I did a lot of remotes from the Harlem YMCA on 135th Street, and I would go outside to talk to the man on the street. When the great tap dancer Bill "Bojangles" Robinson died, I broadcast live from the funeral procession down Broadway, and I did a special tribute to this great entertainer on my morning show. When the Emperor Haile Selassie of Ethiopia visited the United States, I was chosen to ride with him and Mrs. Eleanor Roosevelt to the grave of the late president in Hyde Park upstate, after which I interviewed him for WLIB. We called Emperor Selassie "the Lion of Judah," and everywhere he went crowds of people followed, hoping to catch a glimpse of him. He was like the Nelson Mandela of his day—a symbol of pride and hope for the masses.

Harry Belafonte and Hal during rehearsals for a
Carnegie Hall concert, 1940s

I found Selassie to be an extraordinarily brilliant man, fully versed on international current events. At that time, he was embroiled in a battle with dissidents in his country who were trying to overturn his government. Though he must have been under considerable stress, he never showed it and was always completely dignified and gracious. Selassie dressed in a dark uniform replete with medals and badges and traditional Ethiopian headdress. He was a slight man, around 5 feet, 5 inches tall, but the power radiating from him made him seem larger than life. He wasn't arrogant in any way, but you could feel the sense of importance that surrounded him. He carried himself like royalty at all times.

On the way to the grave site in Hyde Park, we talked a lot about President Roosevelt and the programs he implemented. Mrs. Roosevelt treated Selassie with the utmost respect, and he, in turn, behaved very graciously toward her. She asked a lot of questions about the medical treatment and living conditions of women and children in his homeland. She was always more concerned with children than any of the political maneuverings that might have been going on at the time.

On the radio show, I asked him about his biggest concerns for his country, and he said that Ethiopia needed to focus on economic development. He wanted to get companies to invest and build in the country to create more jobs for the nation's poor. When I asked how he found the United States in comparison to Ethiopia, he said he liked the United States but he wanted to know more about the condition of African Americans. He mentioned the lynchings that had recently occurred down South and questioned whether the federal government would intercede in these cases. And he wanted to know how Black people were holding up in the face of such racism and hostility. All I could say is that we were trying to look to a brighter day.

I enjoyed being in on WLIB's new programming initiative—to reach the Black audience. I was instrumental in bringing Betty Granger to the station. Betty, a columnist for the New York *Amsterdam News,* was also active in the New York Urban League. She had a great personality. When I suggested that she do a daily show on WLIB, she said she was already too busy. But I kept pushing, and I made Harry Novick give her a time slot. I believe I was the first to put a Black woman on the air in New York. We called her show *Breakfast with Betty in The House That Jack Built*. The woman was absolutely terrific—no training, no nothing.

Once I had arrived in New York, I wasted no time in making contacts and establishing relationships. I attracted advertisers to my show and made sure I got a lot of exposure in Harlem with special appearances. I appeared at dozens of benefits and raised some $40,000 for various charities, including the Harlem YMCA. But New York was a big sea and it wasn't easy making a name for myself there. To make matters worse, I found the commute and being away from my family pretty hard to take. I started to get offers from Washington stations, and when my contract with WLIB was up, I decided not to renew.

Instead, I returned to Washington, where I felt I had unfinished business. I learned that Richard Eaton, owner of WOOK, was putting out the word that I owed my success to him, when in fact it was the other way around. I had built WOOK into the most popular station in Washington's Black community. I realized he was still angry with me for unionizing his station, but I didn't like that talk. I decided that the best way for me to prove Eaton wrong was to return to Washington on a competing station.

I had received a good offer even before my contract with WLIB expired. Auto Wholesalers, which had been one of my major sponsors in D.C., approached me with the idea of buying time on a local station for a music show that I would host. They wanted me to help identify the station, create the show's format, and really be in on the ground floor. The challenge appealed to me, and I returned to Washington as soon as I was finished with WLIB. It meant starting over in a lot of ways, but I knew it wouldn't take much time for me to get back into the thick of Washington life.

There was a small station out of Bethesda, Maryland, with the call letters WBCC. The station was nearly bankrupt and the owners were willing to do whatever it took to stay in business. Assured of the backing of Auto Wholesalers, I approached the owners—not just about doing a show but about creating a whole new image for the station. I proposed to move its base of operations from Maryland to U Street in Washington, one of the main streets in the Black community and the center of its night life. U Street was jumping in those days, with clubs and theaters such as the Lincoln, the Republic, and the Booker T. My idea was to build a studio into the front of one of the theaters so that people walking and driving by could look in and see my broadcasting. And I had just the theater in mind. Abe Lichtman, my old partner from the Washington Bears days, just happened to own the Republic. When I proposed to Abe that we build a studio in his theater, he liked the idea, and gave his okay. The owners of WBCC also went along with it, and agreed to change the call letters of the station to WUST, for U Street.

Once I had put all that in place, I concentrated on the format of the show. By this time, the number of programs aimed at D.C.'s Black market had grown, and I wanted to find a way to distinguish my new show from the other music shows on the air. So I thought about what interested the average Black Washingtonian: jobs, housing, education, and equal fights were high on the list, of course. But all those things involved struggle. In fact, the day-to-day life of the average Black Washingtonian was a struggle. To escape from the realities of their lives, they did a lot of dreaming about striking it rich, and the biggest dream they had was to hit the numbers. Washington, D.C., had one of the biggest numbers rackets in the country.

The numbers were—and still are—illegal. Nowadays, you have all these city and state lotteries and legal numbers games; but the illegal numbers, which allow poor people to place small bets on the chance of making big money, still flourish. You choose three numbers, in various combinations, and place your bet that your numbers will win. The illegal numbers racket supports a variety of related businesses, including fortune–tellers, the publishers of *Lucky Numbers Dream Books*, and the like. The winning numbers are determined in various ways, but at that time in Washington, D.C., they were derived from horse racing results. So I decided to appeal to the dreams of Black Washingtonians by reporting the horse racing results on my show.

I named my four-hour show, which broadcast 1 to 5 P.M. each day, *The Sports Page*, and included nationwide horse racing results in between music selections and commercials. I had a horse racing ticker installed right there in the broadcasting booth—the first and only one of its kind in Washington. I never mentioned the numbers on the air, but listeners knew that when I said, "In a moment we'll be bringing you the results of the first race from Tanforan, California," they had time to get a pencil and paper ready to write the number down. Within four months, WUST was in the black—for the first time since 1946—and my show was one of the highest rated in the region. Two months later, the show hit the number one spot, and I had succeeded in showing Richard Eaton and the others at WOOK that they had not made me; the credit was all mine.

By this time I was back on the charity circuit. One of my big causes was better housing for Blacks in Washington. Under segregation, Blacks were forced to live in overcrowded and substandard housing in the poor sections of town. A fair-housing movement had gotten underway after World War II, and I used my position as a local celebrity both on and off the air to urge people to put pressure on the authorities to change the situation. I led picket lines and visited demonstrations to give my support.

Another cause to which I devoted a lot of time was a summer jobs program for Black youth, who often languished—and got into trouble—during the summer because they had nothing to do. I called and visited many local businesses and urged them to hire these young people. I announced the names of businesses that agreed to participate in the program on the air. This was like a free commercial for them. I managed to get summer jobs for several thousand youngsters in that way. They didn't earn much money, but it was enough to buy some clothes for school or to help out their families, and it kept them off the street doing something productive.

Word of the jobs program somehow reached President Truman, and I was invited to the White House, where the president presented me with a beautiful scroll in recognition of my work on behalf of Washington's young people. At the time, I told the president that I would like to interview him on my show someday, and he said he would be glad to do it, but we didn't make any specific plans.

After going back to Washington, I also returned to the broadcast booth at Howard University, doing the play-by-play for both football and baseball games. In 1951, I was invited to host Howard's commencement exercises and broadcast them live from the campus. President Truman just happened to be the featured speaker, and when I reminded him of his promise to go on my show, he said, "Well, why don't we just take a few minutes right now and talk?" So, right there, we talked about sports at Howard as well as about local issues. I was amazed at how much the president knew about what was going on in Washington's Black community. After the interview, Truman gave his commencement address and, to my surprise, concluded by calling me forward and presenting me with a plaque. It was one of the proudest moments of my life.

FREE

every **SATURDAY** & **SUNDAY** *Afternoon*

the ampeg sound

PRESENTS

TOP RECORDING STARS
IN PERSON

record world ◯ ⊕ SHOW

PRODUCED BY
RADIO & TV PERSONALITY

HAL JACKSON

AT

PALISADES
AMUSEMENT PARK N.J.

HALF MILE SOUTH OF

GEO WASHINGTON BRIDGE

also **SATURDAYS 3-5 P.M.**

BROADCASTS LIVE DIRECT

6.

BACK TO THE BIG APPLE

hings were going well for me at WUST, and I had no interest in making another move. But one day a big, chauffeured limousine pulled up in front of the WUST broadcast booth. Nathan Strauss, owner of WMCA, the largest independent radio station in New York City, stepped out. He was there to invite me to go to New York.

I told him I'd already been there.

"But not on a station like WMCA," he pointed out, and he was right. WMCA, 570 on the dial, had an open signal, which meant that it had 360-degree coverage instead of being beamed in just one direction. WLIB had been barely able to reach Harlem; WMCA could be heard as far south as Atlantic City and well north into upstate New York.

Strauss continued his sales pitch to me. He wanted me to return to New York not as a Black personality but as a personality, period. He didn't expect me to adopt the persona of Black emcees like Hippy Joe or Dr. Jive, nor did he expect the jazzy delivery that went along with such names. He would let me keep my dignity. He said he liked the way I conducted myself on the air and believed that I would appeal equally to Black and White listeners. The show he wanted me to do would be called *The All-American Revue*. I liked the inclusive sound of that title. I also liked Nathan Strauss, a fine man with strong principles. In all my years of knowing him I never saw him compromise those principles.

Nathan Strauss was also a smart businessman. His advertising and promotion people had conducted a study on "New York's Negro Market," as they put it in a promotional brochure they produced to announce my return to the Big Apple. The brochure advised that in metropolitan New York:

One MILLION twelve thousand eight hundred and eighty-three (1,012,883) Negroes spend one BILLION two hundred fifty million dollars ($1,250,000,000) every year.

- Income of the average Negro family has TRIPLED in the past ten years
- Scope of Negroes employment is almost unlimited
- More than 200,000 new homes now occupied or being readied for occupancy by Negro families
- Standard of living for Negroes is at an all-time high

More Negroes than ever before are in the market for
- MORE HOUSEHOLD APPLIANCES
- MORE AUTOMOBILES

· MORE CLOTHING
· MORE FURNITURE
In addition to more foods, drugs, beverages and other
better nationally advertised products . . . both the ne-
cessities and luxuries which go with good living.

The salary Strauss offered me was not high, $300 or $350 a
week, as I recall. But as was customary, it included a percentage

*Piano great Bud Powell and trumpeter Dizzy Gillespie with Hal
backstage at Birdland, 1948*

of the advertising revenue I secured. WMCA had an established sales department and a hefty list of sponsors, so I wouldn't have to beat the bushes for advertising; but I would benefit from whatever sponsorship I did attract. I decided to accept Nathan Strauss's offer. Once again, my family preferred to stay in Washington, so, in 1954, I moved up by myself and got an apartment in the Ivey Delph, an exclusive apartment complex at 19 Hamilton Terrace, just off 141st Street in the Striver's Row section of Harlem.

Hamilton Terrace was a sloping, tree-lined side street with rows of beautifully kept brownstones, some of which boasted intricately patterned stained-glass windows. Ornate, wrought-iron street lamps were interspersed with tall, white-blossomed trees up and down the street. I could look out of my front door to the left at Morningside Park and, on the northwest corner of the street, St. Luke's Church. St. Luke's was a huge brick church, almost a full block long, with massive rounded turrets and blue and purple oblong-shaped stained-glass windows. It sat on the same property as the Hamilton Grange National Memorial, home of Alexander Hamilton from 1802 to 1804. It was a bright yellow, three-story Southern-style home that reminded me very much of my childhood home back in South Carolina. The Ivey Delph occupied a choice spot at the corner nearest St. Luke's.

After a year, my family finally joined me in New York. With so much to do and see, the children were enthralled. They especially loved the West Indian street vendors who sold sugar cane and coconuts and pomegranates on the corner in our neighborhood. Julia immediately became very friendly with

HJ spinning records at WOOK, Washington, D.C.

Gabby Hayes and Edward Muldare with HJ

Clockwise from bottom left, Hal, Johnny Hartman, Billy Erskine, George Treadwell, Timmie Rodgers, and Sarah Vaughan at Birdland, 1954

Rose Morgan, the wife of Joe Louis. Rose owned Rose Morgan's House of Beauty, a salon on 145th Street around the corner from our apartment. Painted in eye-catching hot pink, it was hard to miss, and everyone who was anyone came to Rose Morgan's to have their hair, nails, and face done. Through Joe and Rose, my family became connected to all the movers and shakers in Harlem.

A few months later, in 1955, the entire family moved to

199th Avenue in St. Albans, Queens—everyone except Jane, who by then was on her own and working as a teacher in the Washington, D.C., school system. I continued living in the Ivey Delph during the week and commuted to St. Albans on weekends. In St. Albans, we had a two-family, five-bedroom house with a parlor, living room, full dining room, and eat-in kitchen both upstairs and downstairs. My wife and I lived downstairs where there were three bedrooms, and my mother-in-law, Ercer, lived upstairs.

Mother-in-law jokes were big among comedians at that time, and I took advantage of their popularity and started telling a lot of my own. This did not endear me to Julia's mother, but it gave my fans something to say to me on the street. "How's your mother-in-law?" they'd call out. Tommy Edwards even wrote a song about her, entitled "Paging Mr. Jackson," that sold well locally.

My return to New York was greeted with a rash of publicity, courtesy of WMCA's big advertising and promotions department. There were billboards and ads and promotional pieces on WMCA. I still have a copy of the promotional booklet they issued that described the format of my new show.

> The "All-American Revue" offers the best in American musical entertainment . . . a program featuring top artists of all races, creeds and colors. . . . With strong appeal to every community in Metropolitan New York . . . another plus in WMCA's popular program format. Witness Duke Ellington, Sarah Vaughan, Frank Sinatra, Xavier Cugat . . . all members of the great team of American entertainers. . . .

Community leaders, clergymen and outstanding personalities in public life will team up in "All American Revue." The top entertainment qualities of the program format will be supplemented nightly by a brief "Message of the Day," featuring local leaders well-known to all New Yorkers and respected everywhere.

Hal, Sammy Davis Jr., and his wife, Mai Brett, raising funds for the Harlem YMCA *at the Savoy Ballroom, 1950s*

That pretty much sets forth the format of the show, which was broadcast nightly from 8 to 10 P.M. I selected my own records, and it was great to be able to play the music of the top White musicians and singers without worrying about the reaction of the station owners. WMCA's record library was tops, and I played Montavani and Tony Bennett as well as Arthur Prysock and Ella Fitzgerald. Through the Message of the Day, I got to know many of the city politicians and leaders, which came in handy when I started doing fund-raisers and other activities for worthy causes.

In the beginning, I spent a great deal of my off-air time developing sponsors. Working with the WMCA sales department, I would identify potential new sponsors and then contact them to sell them advertising time. In some instances, I also helped the sponsor. This was the case with Parks Sausage, founded by Henry G. Parks.

Parks was an interesting guy, born in Atlanta but raised in Ohio, where his parents moved during the migration north around World War I. Henry always wanted to be in business for himself, but at Ohio State a placement counselor told him that if he wanted to be a success in business he should do two things: change his name and go to South America to acquire a Spanish accent. The counselor believed that Parks had a much greater chance of success if he passed himself off as a Latino businessman than as an African American. But Parks replied that he would not run from anything, least of all from himself.

By the time Parks graduated from Ohio State, the United States was gearing up for World War II. He worked for a time with Dr. Mary McLeod Bethune at the Resident War Production Training Center in Wilberforce, Ohio. He then moved to New York, where he owned and operated several businesses, including a theatrical booking agency. He also attempted to form a soft-drink company with the great Black boxing champion, Joe Louis; the product was to be called Joe Louis Punch. This turned out to be a very big business.

Relocating to Baltimore, at various times Parks owned a drugstore, dealt in real estate, and operated a cement-block plant. In 1951, believing that there was a market for Southern-style sausage in Baltimore's Black community, he and several others founded Parks Sausage Company. They adapted an old Virginia recipe to mass production techniques and set up a plant and their offices in a rented building. Six people ran the whole operation. Henry Parks was the chief marketer.

Parks managed to get a big supermarket contract in Washington, D.C., but he was having trouble breaking into the New York market: the chain stores were just not open to a Black manufacturer. I came up with the idea of going directly to the public. After I got the Parks Sausage advertising contract, I arranged for Henry to hire nice-looking young women in white uniforms to stand in front of the big chain stores like A&P and Safeway. They had platters of cooked sausage slices on toothpicks and offered free samples. I would take my microphone and interview the samplers about how they liked the sausage. I would even ask trivia questions and give free theater tickets to the winners.

Parks Sausage was delicious, and giving out samples and interviewing the people on the street created a demand for the product that the grocery stores had to fill if they were going to keep their customers happy. It also caused people to tune in to my show to hear themselves or their friends interviewed on the air. It was a history-making campaign. Parks Sausage conquered New York, as it did the rest of the eastern seaboard. In 1969, Parks Sausage became the first Black-owned business to offer its stock for public trading. By 1971, the company had contracts with every major East Coast supermarket chain, most of them in White suburbs, and annual sales of more than $10 million.

Millions of Americans knew of Parks Sausage through a memorable advertisement in which a little boy calls, "More Parks Sausages, Mom . . . pleeeease?" Very few people realized that the company was Black-owned.

Sadly, the company went down after Henry Parks died; but I am pleased that football great Franco Harris is trying to rescue the company, and I hope he succeeds.

I had not been back in New York long before I was all over the dial, just as I had been in Washington. About two months after I went on the air over WMCA, I was approached by Al Lamphian about doing a show for WNJR out of Newark. Al had been general manager at WOOK in Washington, and we had remained friends in spite of the troubles there. The Rollins broadcasting chain out of Atlanta had recruited Al to come to Newark and turn WNJR into a Black-oriented station. He had already recruited Georgie Hudson to do a morning show, but he needed an established personality to help him attract the afternoon audience. He invited me to do a show in the 4 to 6 P.M. slot.

When I approached Nathan Strauss about the offer, he had

no objections. WNJR was a small station and no competition for WMCA. So I agreed to help Al out. I didn't take the job for the money, because Al couldn't afford to pay me much. I took it because I liked the idea of being the only disc jockey in the New York area working on more than one station.

Then, about a month after I went on the air over WNJR, Morris Levy called me. He had taken over the nightclub Birdland from Monty Kay, who was Diahann Carroll's husband and manager at the time. Under Monty Kay, the midnight show at Birdland had been broadcast live every night over WABC. The emcee was Symphony Sid. But Symphony Sid left for Boston to do another live show from the club called Storyville. Morris Levy, whom everyone called Mush, wanted me to take Sid's place.

I jumped at the offer. WABC was a network, and no other Black broadcast over a network station. For the first time, I would have a national audience. I had to get the okay from Nathan Strauss, of course, but again he had no objection because the show did not present any major competition for the shows he had in that time slot. Nathan Strauss said to me, "Fine, if you can hold up physically."

That was a consideration. I was taking on a lot. The show over WABC was six hours, midnight to 6 A.M., which meant that I would have very little time for sleep. But I couldn't leave Al Lamphian, and I couldn't leave WMCA. So I decided to work all three shows. And so it was that I became the first New York radio personality to have daily radio shows on three separate stations.

Only the first hour of the show was broadcast live from Birdland. At 1 A.M. we went over to the studio, which held

Hal with Billie Holiday and Dizzy Gillespie
at Carnegie Hall, 1950s

about 300 people, and from there we would record a music-and-interview show. The audience would drift in and out all night, and so would the big-name celebrities who happened to be in town. Between the broadcast from Birdland and the broadcast from the ABC studios, I got to work with many of the big artists of the day—Stan Kenton, Charlie Parker, Nat Cole, Billy Eckstein, Sarah Vaughan, Dizzy Gillespie, Billie Holiday.

Dinah Washington was a regular on the show. She talked all bad, but she had a really soft heart. I remember running into

Tina Turner backstage just minutes before she was supposed to perform. Her face was bloody from a run-in with Ike Turner, but by the time they went on she had fixed herself up with makeup. I loved the woman—she was determined not to let Ike or life defeat her.

In the studio show, we talked about a variety of music and artists, then I'd play the records. The famous Stage Delicatessen provided food for my guests and me in exchange for an on-air plug. It was basically a hosting job. Morris Levy handled the other matters, such as selling time and booking acts. But there was still a lot to do, what with interviews, record announcements, and commercials.

After about a month, Morris allowed me to hire someone to help me pull records and do whatever else I needed done. A young man named Telly Savalas got the job. He was just starting out and really didn't know how to go about pursuing a career in show business; when he wasn't busy helping with the show, he was always writing scripts. He was a smart guy. But he was lazy, and I told him so. I told him to get an agent and even offered to put in a word for him at the William Morris Agency, with which I had an association through some of the major beer companies that were sponsors of my various radio shows. One morning after the show ended, Telly and I had breakfast and then he went over to the William Morris Agency. They agreed to represent him, and his career took off from there.

That Birdland show was a great success. Initially broadcast locally, the live part of the show was soon picked up by the ABC network and, at one time, it was carried by fifty-four stations across the country. *Life* magazine did a report on it and said that we had the largest radio audience in the world, some 7 to 10 million listeners. Some of the stations also carried the five-hour show from the studio. There were about twenty telephones in the studio, and calls came from listeners across the country, and even as far away as South America. Mail came in from all over the world. Many of those listeners did not know I was Black, and with that show I really proved Nathan Strauss's belief that I could appeal to a wide audience.

Later I learned that it wasn't just members of the audience who didn't realize I was Black; some of the ABC executives didn't know it either. I remember some of them came in while I was on the air and did a double-take. They had been listening to the show and enjoying it, but only when they saw me did they realize I was Black.

It was an extremely hectic schedule. I had the morning and evening shows over WMCA, the afternoon show over WNJR six days a week, and the Birdland show seven nights a week. The only free time I had was on Sundays. But when a local television station, WPIX, which was owned by the *New York Daily News*, approached me about doing a Sunday morning children's show, I took it.

Even though I was usually absent during the week, I tried to discipline and guide my children. I'd call every day and talk to them. Sunday had been the one day when we got together and spent time enjoying ourselves.

I didn't make the decision lightly, since that had been my family day. On Sundays, the children, Julia, and I would attend an early-morning church service and then come back home and enjoy a huge family breakfast that my wife and mother-in-law prepared. In the afternoons, I took the children out to do whatever they wanted. We explored New York from end to end, taking in movies or shows, going to museums, the zoos, the parks, and anyplace else they could dream up. I cherished whatever time I could grab with my children because they were growing up so quickly. Jane had already moved out, and my son, Hal Junior, had recently enrolled at Groton Academy in Massachusetts. He came home on the weekends as much as possible, but I could still see the time slipping away from us. Only my youngest daughter, Jewell, was still at home.

Television was still basically off-limits to Blacks, except for Eddie "Rochester" Anderson on *The Jack Benny Show* and those few occasions when a great star, such as Paul Robeson or Marian Anderson, appeared on a special. In the end, I decided to do the show because I saw it as a chance to open another door.

Uncle Hal's Kiddie Show was a showcase for talented youngsters of all races presented before a live studio audience that was fully integrated. There was no script. The producers selected the kids who were to appear on the show, and I would talk to them a bit and then introduce their performances. Leslie Uggams got her first break on my show. She was about 8 or 9 years old and just brimming with talent. As "Uncle Hal, the Kiddies' Pal," I really enjoyed the opportunity to showcase the talent of these youngsters. *Uncle Hal's Kiddie Show* stayed on the air for twenty-six weeks.

I had hoped that this foray into television would set the stage for a bigger break. I still dreamed of being on national television, and my biggest dream was doing sports broadcasting nationally. Although I was now based in New York, I continued to take time off every year to do the play-by-play for a couple of the big Black collegiate athletic contests. I announced the famous football duels between Howard University and Lincoln University, which alternated between Washington and Philadelphia and which were sponsored by Lincoln-Mercury. I also took time off every year to announce the Colored Intercollegiate Athletic Association football championship game in Washington. The "Capital Classic" drew between 30,000 and 35,000 spectators to Griffith Stadium every year, and I believed the games would draw a national audience if broadcast over network television.

To this end, I started talking to ABC network executives about putting the games on the air, and they were interested. So were the presidents of the Black colleges. But the NCAA had other ideas. When word about what I was trying to do got out, the NCAA threatened to suspend the Black schools involved. The NCAA had a contract with NBC, which broadcast one game a week, and they weren't going to let anybody broadcast on ABC. I pointed out that the Black college contests were almost never televised—you'd get an occasional broadcast of a Capital Classic, but those televised games on Saturdays were almost exclusively of White college contests. But that didn't persuade them. An NCAA official named Bucknell was dead-set on keeping Black colleges off the air, and he wouldn't budge. His final words were that if any of the Black colleges went on ABC-TV with me, they would be thrown out of the NCAA, because their rule was only one network. That would mean that Black athletes would be barred from integrated track meets like the Penn Relays—the only contests that the NCAA had allowed to be integrated so far.

ABC's position was that they would stand by their three-year deal with me. We already had the sponsors lined up. The Black college presidents were ready to defy the NCAA, but I feared the repercussions on the schools. Black college teams were just beginning to get recognition in the NCAA. I decided to drop the project.

I still kept up the pressure on the NCAA to allow Black college bowl games to be televised. When that finally happened a couple of years later, I felt that I could take at least some of the credit. The NCAA still only puts about two Black college contests on a year—usually Grambling games.

That was not the only disappointment I suffered in the area of sports broadcasting. If Bill Veeck had been allowed to buy the Baltimore Orioles, I would have become the announcer for them. I had Bill's promise that if the deal went through, I would have the job. But according to the rules of the American League, not only did the previous owner and the new owner have to agree on a price but the other owners in the league also had to approve the transfer of a team from one owner to another. Bill was known to favor integration, and I think the other owners were afraid he would bring too many Black players to Baltimore. He was turned down.

Later, Bill bought the Cleveland Indians and signed Larry Doby, Satchel Paige, and several other old-timers who had starred in the Negro Leagues. But I'd lost my chance to be the first Black play-by-play announcer in the major leagues.

In the 1950s, I came very close to becoming the play-by-

play announcer for the New York Yankees. I had the sponsorship of Ballantine beer lined up, and the backing of the
William Morris Agency. I did several demo tapes. But at the
last moment, the Yankees' front office backed out. They just
weren't ready for a Black announcer. Word had leaked out that
I would be signed, and to avoid the anger of their very large
Black audience, the Yankees signed Roy Campanella to host
the half-time show at double-headers. Roy was in a wheelchair
by this time, and that job gave him a much-needed boost; but
it was a great disappointment for me.

Figuring that I was not going to get on television as a sports
announcer, I decided to try a different route. That's when I
came up with the idea for a variety show. I called it *Hal Jackson's American Beauties*. The major departure was that in addition to top musical stars, it would also showcase beautiful and
talented young Black women, who would handle the commercials and also help me introduce the stars. At that time, no
major network was using Black models to sell merchandise.
ABC liked the idea, and Ford Motor Company agreed to sponsor it. I spent months recruiting and training the girls. But we
ran into trouble with the local affiliates. Few stations would
agree to air a show with a Black emcee that featured beautiful
Black women. Only two stations agreed to carry the show. De-
spite the backing of the network and full sponsorship of the
show by Ford, we had to cancel about a month before scheduled air time. That was a big disappointment. Looking back, I
understand that it was another idea of mine that was ahead of
its time. America just wasn't ready for *Hal Jackson's American
Beauties*.

7.

WLIB AND THE PAYOLA SCANDAL

By 1955, after three years with WMCA, I was ready for a change. I had established exclusive relationships with several big sponsors, but I was still getting the same, comparatively small percentage of what amounted to about $200,000 worth of advertising. Also, by this time the civil rights movement was really gearing up—the Montgomery, Alabama, bus strike started that year—and I wanted to do more for that cause, but I was hampered by my "All-American Revue" image. I wanted to do more programming aimed at Black listeners, and I couldn't do that on WMCA. So when Nat Ruddick, general manager of WLIB, the station that had brought me to New York City the first time, approached me with an offer, I was willing to listen.

By this time, owner Harry Novick had built WLIB into a much stronger station. Back in 1949, it had a 1,000-watt signal. Now, it had a 10,000-watt transmitter on the Long Island waterfront that could reach New York, New Jersey, and Con-

Hal with Frankie Valli and the Four Seasons
and an event hostess, 1950s

necticut. There was no more foreign-language programming
on the station: it was now all Black-oriented programming.
Betty Granger from *The Amsterdam News,* whom I had
brought on during my first stint with the station, was still there.
Buddy Bowser and Sarah Lou Harris cohosted another show.

Nat Ruddick met my salary demands and my insistence on
a larger percentage of the advertising I brought in. He also
agreed that I could keep working for WNJR and continue to do
the Birdland show for ABC. With all that in place, I signed the
contract and looked forward to doing shows aimed specifically
at the Black audience.

I did a morning show from sunrise to 10 A.M., and then an
afternoon show from 3 P.M. to sign-off (WLIB was still a daytime station). For the morning show, I returned *The House That*

Jack Built to the airwaves. The afternoon show was a sports show.

By the time I rejoined WLIB, a lot of programming was aimed at Black audiences or featured Black music. By this time, it was no longer called "race music"; instead, it was called rhythm and blues, but it was still Black music. A lot of disc jockeys on small local stations specialized in it. Tommy "Dr. Jive" Smalls had a show over WWRL; Jocko Henderson, whose New York career I was instrumental in launching, was on WOV; Willie Bryant and Ray Carroll cohosted a late-night R&B show on WHOM from the Baby Grand on West 125th Street, and Bill Cooke did *Cookie's Caravan* on WAAT out of Newark. Phil Gordon, William B. Williams, and Fred Robbins were all on the same station doing R&B shows. Fred did his *Robbins' Nest* remotes from a Broadway club called the Royal Roost. But WLIB more than held its own against all that competition, partly because of my efforts to bring R&B to other arenas.

Through the Birdland show, I had made contacts with a lot of the jazz venues in New York. Jazz was really hot in New York during the 1950s. The clubs on West 52nd Street, one block of which has since been officially named "Swing Street," featured the big names, like Sarah Vaughan, Billy Taylor, Mary Lou Williams, Dizzy Gillespie, and Billie Holiday. I emceed a series of jazz concerts at Carnegie Hall put on by Morris Levy with a lot of those jazz greats.

I got to know Billie through my Birdland show; in fact, I spent a lot of time with her. She was wonderful talent, but she was not easy to work with. There was one time when she was

Poster for the first ever rock' n' roll show at Carnegie Hall, 1950s

supposed to open a Carnegie Hall show. By curtain time she had not shown up, so I had to scramble to rearrange the schedule of acts. Stan Kenton, Nat King Cole, and Duke Ellington were on the same program. Then, at about 11:30 P.M., I went to the back door to take one last look, and here comes Billie.

"You gonna bust me?" she wanted to know.

"No, I'm not," I said. "Come on and get on stage!"

Well, that lady took the stage and sang her heart out. When she finished, you could have heard a pin drop. Whatever you had to go through with Billie was worth the trouble.

I first became aware of the preponderance of drug use among Black entertainers at Birdland. I'd see musicians shooting up, thinking it would make them able to play all night. They did play all night, but at a terrible cost to their bodies. With so many other handicaps, dope was one that we could do without, so I started antidrug programs for young people, hoping to reach them before they got hooked. My slogan was simple: "If you haven't tried drugs, don't start; if you are on drugs, get off!" I organized a series of programs in high schools. I brought in rehabilitated addicts to talk to the students and offered them a chance for counseling and treatment, no questions asked. I found that the students were interested in my life story, about how I had succeeded against the odds, and I spoke to many groups of high school students about working hard and applying yourself. In one year alone, I made more than 150 appearances at high schools.

By the middle 1950s, postwar prosperity had found its way to the record business. The old 78-rpm records were giving way to the 45s, which were lighter, more durable, easier to make and distribute. From a disc jockey's point of view, they were also a lot easier to handle and play. The wartime shortages of shellac that had drastically reduced the production of new records was over, and a lot of new record companies were starting. Many of these companies were Black, or White-owned but featuring Black music. There was a big market for R&B among young people, and record companies were quick to capitalize on it.

In those days, a lot of recordings were "covers." One singer would come out with a song on record, and if it was popular, the record companies would release the same song recorded by another singer. After R&B got big, the big record companies would get White stars to record covers of Black stars' records. Little Willie John recorded "Fever" in 1956, two years before Peggy Lee's version, but it was hers that went to the top of the charts. A lot of White producers would go to the Apollo Theater and secretly record the Black performers, then release the same songs by White artists.

But gradually the Black stars were getting more exposure

and more opportunities to record. The Chess Record Company in Chicago was a pioneer in this area. It had contracts with Muddy Waters, Howlin' Wolf, and Chuck Berry before it signed Bo Diddley. Chess released Chuck Berry's "Maybelline" in 1955, and it went on to win *Billboard* magazine's triple award for that year—biggest rhythm and blues record, biggest rhythm and blues record on the radio stations, and most played rhythm and blues record on jukeboxes. That same year, Chess issued Bo Diddley's first record, "Bo Diddley" / "I'm a Man" and his career really took off.

Diddley's distinctive guitar playing, with its driving, "basic bottom" beat, was soon being imitated by both White and Black performers. When a young kid from Tennessee named Elvis Presley made his first trip to New York, he went straight to the Apollo Theater. He saw Bo Diddley drive the audience crazy with his hip-gyrating performance. Buddy Holly, another young White performer out of Texas, incorporated Diddley's double-rhythm guitar pattern into his playing.

Although White performers had been tapping into Black music for quite a while, mainstream White audiences had still not been introduced to rhythm and blues on a large scale. That all changed with the coming of Alan Freed. He became the first White disc jockey to break radio's unwritten color line by playing R&B on a White station—and a big White station at that.

I met Alan through Morris Levy. Alan, who was from Cleveland, began doing a recorded show for WNJR in Newark, and it became an instant hit in the New York market. Morris heard about it and brought Freed to New York to produce a live music show. That show at the Paramount Theater in

Brooklyn in September 1954 featured Fats Domino, Chuck Berry, Dionne Warwick, and the Crystals and attracted 15,000 people, 10,000 of whom had to be turned away.

The following week, Freed was offered a time slot on WINS, which is now an all-news station but was then one of the pioneer White stations playing R&B.

WWRL *Christmas collection for the poor in Harlem, 1950s*

When Alan moved to WINS, he came with the assumption that he would be able to use his Cleveland radio name, "The Moondog." But there was a guy already working in New York on Broadway who used the name Moondog. I was in the studio with Alan his second night on the air when, right before the start of the show, the other guy's lawyer came and served papers on him. Effective immediately, Alan could no longer use the name Moondog. With just a few minutes until airtime, he suddenly had no name for his show. Alan didn't know what to do. The first song of the night was a Bo Diddley tune. Then the song ended and it was time for Alan to announce himself.

Finally Alan said, "Well, I don't know, man. We can keep playing records, and we can keep rockin' and rollin' all night."

From then on, Alan's show was called "The Alan Freed Rock and Roll Show." And that was the first time the term "rock and roll" was used.

Alan was a very open-minded and liberal person, the one White person who really reached out to give Black artists real exposure. I really liked him and didn't feel that we were in competition because he had his audience, which was mostly White, and I had mine. Having him in the New York area was actually good for me, because he was enlarging the market for the kind of music I was promoting. We did a lot of benefits together, and they were integrated—both the acts and the audiences. We really had the backing of a lot of people.

Alan just had a way of drawing people in, and he never played the race card. The kids were just kids to him. He didn't care if they were Black kids or White kids. Of course, some people didn't like that. And when he got his television show going, they really hated it. But he was so powerful by then that no one could do anything to stop him.

Still, the resistance to R&B and rock 'n' roll didn't go away. I guess rock 'n' roll presented a real threat because it was so obviously derived from Black roots but was still popular among White kids. Many established recording stars spoke out against rock 'n' roll, Frank Sinatra among them. Nat King Cole even recorded a song called "Mr. Cole Won't Rock 'n' Roll." A lot of the White radio station owners were against it, too. In retrospect, it wasn't surprising that the establishment would look for a way to stop what was going on.

Meanwhile, rhythm and blues grew more popular every day. With that in mind, I approached Carnegie Hall officials about doing an R&B concert, but they turned me down flat; R&B had an undeservedly bad reputation. It was considered decadent music by a lot of people, and it still wasn't played on the big stations in New York. One reason I chafed at WMCA was that I was not allowed to play R&B on my *All-American Revue* show.

When it came to live performances, there was even more concern on the part of the powers that be. Like rock 'n' roll later on, R&B was regarded as potentially inflammatory music that would attract the wrong kind of crowd, one that might become unruly.

Still, I kept pushing the Carnegie Hall management to let me book Fats Domino for a show. I pointed to my previous concerts at the hall and gave assurances that I would arrange for adequate security. Finally they agreed, and in 1957 I brought in a show headlined by Fats Domino and about eight other acts.

Dorothy Kilgallen, the influential New York *Herald-American* columnist, helped publicize that show. She devoted an entire column to it and even attended the show, sitting right up there in the front row. When I asked her why she had been so helpful, she said, "Hal, I've got people watching you, and you do a lot of beautiful things in this town." The show was a smash, attracting a large audience of Blacks and Whites who never once got out of hand. Carnegie Hall gave R&B the official stamp of approval, and some of the DJs on the big White radio stations started giving it a little airtime. It was what kids wanted to hear. But there was still a lot of opposition from the big station owners, who feared that R&B would scare away sponsors or cause the advertising rates to go down if the sponsors thought the stations were sounding "too Black."

On WLIB, I didn't have that problem, and I played a lot of R&B. It was around this time that I met Berry Gordy. He had a job working on a Detroit assembly line but was starting out in the music business, writing songs for Jackie Wilson and others. He and Marv Johnson came by the WLIB studio just to say hello, and Berry and I took to each other immediately. He was a quiet, soft-spoken guy, but he had a big ambition to create his

Hal with Margaret Jackson and NAACP *chief Roy Wilkins during annual* NAACP *fashion show, 1950s*

own sound and build up his own acts. By the end of the 1950s, he had opened his Hitsville USA studios in three converted residential buildings in Detroit and had a group of young local artists whom he was developing into stars. He took the straight, driving, R&B beat that sold just among Black people and turn it into something that appealed to the White pop audience, too.

I'd begun organizing Saturday afternoon dances at the Rockland Palace on 155th Street and Eighth Avenue in Harlem, and I always featured R&B at those sets. The dances were benefits for the Harlem YMCA, which was one of my pet causes. They also filled a need in the community, because the young people had very few events to go to. Under my agreement with the Y, I did the promoting and hosting, and the Y provided hostesses and security and handled the money. The dances were a huge success. At the time, Latin music was really popular, and I would usually bring in a Latin band like the late Tito Puente's, along with a rhythm and blues band. I also had popular recording stars come in to lip-sync their records. We drew between 4,000 and 5,000 young people every Saturday, and we rarely had a problem with crowd control. The Y had parent volunteers supervising the streets outside the Rockland Palace.

At first, the police tried to harass the kids as they left the hall, accusing them of being drunk and disorderly. But we didn't serve any liquor at those dances and were careful about checking what the kids brought in, so we knew it was a case of police harassment. We complained at the precinct level, and when that didn't end the problem, we went all the way to

Mayor Robert Wagner, who was very cooperative and helped straighten the whole matter out. Those dances raised about $200,000 for the Harlem Y.

I also hosted a lot of benefits at the Savoy Ballroom for Harry Novick's favorite charities. They were held on Friday nights, and, usually, I didn't finish until 3 or 4 A.M. Afterward, I went straight to the studio in Long Island for my sunrise show. I'd sleep on a table in the studio until it was time to go on the air. The studio had a cement floor, and, in the wintertime, it was so cold I'd have to broadcast with my coat on. My family and I were living on Long Island by that time. In winter, when I heard that snow was forecast, I'd have to leave for the station late in the evening to avoid the snowdrifts, which were sometimes deep enough to bury cars, and arrive before sunrise.

I didn't complain. That was the way things were for Black disc jockeys into those days. At least I was able to play the kind of music I wanted to play, and, just as important, I could really involve myself in the Black community. Frank Schiffman, owner of the Apollo Theater on 125th Street, was always asking me to host the shows there, and I did them as often as my schedule permitted. I enjoyed doing those shows, and they only increased my visibility in the Black community and built my listenership. WLIB claimed (and had the ratings figures to back up that claim) to have "more Negro listeners than any other metropolitan New York station—network or independent."

But as the 1950s wore on, the distinctions between White and Black music and White and Black audiences were disappearing. Not surprisingly, the change was taking place just as Blacks began to win their battle for equality.

The success of the bus boycott in Montgomery, Alabama, opened the floodgates to the nonviolent civil rights movement and catapulted a young Baptist minister named Martin Luther King Jr. to national fame. I began supporting Martin's Southern Christian Leadership Conference a few months after the boycott ended. My involvement started when I took a trip to Washington in the mid-1950s. Martin was there, and when we met, he pulled me aside and said, "Hal, I know what you're doing in New York. Do you think you could help us raise some funds? We're struggling." I promised to help out, and over the next ten years I helped arrange fund-raisers for the SCLC whenever I could. During that time, I got to know Martin very well.

I was with him in 1958 when he was autographing copies of his first book, *Stride Toward Freedom*, at Blumstein's department store in Harlem. Suddenly, a deranged woman ran up and started screaming that he was a communist and was trying to convert her to Catholicism. Without warning, she pulled a letter opener out of her pocket and plunged it into his chest!

We rushed him to Harlem Hospital, where doctors removed the blade, which had come so close to his heart that it could have caused massive hemorrhaging and death. The thing that impressed me most throughout the whole episode was Martin's calm. He remained fully alert; he never panicked. In fact, he tried to reassure us. He kept telling us not to worry, that he would be all right. After his condition was stabilized, his first concern was for his attacker, Mrs. Izola Curry. He realized she was sick and didn't want to press charges against her.

When interviewed later, Mrs. Curry repeated her claims

that Martin was an antireligious communist. She was totally confused; it seems she thought that Martin was the head of the NAACP. She was later committed to a state hospital for the criminally insane.

It was also in the late 1950s that I got to know Malcolm X, the charismatic minister of Muslim Temple No. 7 in Harlem. I interviewed him quite a few times while broadcasting from the Hotel Theresa on WLIB and on WWRL. Malcolm was always candid when discussing his agenda for African Americans, his struggle to gain respect for Blacks in this country. He wanted Blacks to accept and act on a renewed sense of self-worth and dignity. He hated the second-class-citizen mentality, and he wouldn't even talk to you if he felt you were still groveling and talking that old junk.

As my friendship with Malcolm developed, he would often speak to me about Elijah Muhammad and the Nation of Islam. But the closer we got, the more it seemed to me that he wasn't looking to Elijah for guidance as much as Elijah was looking to him. Sometimes we spoke about sports and less serious things, but Malcolm had a way of always bringing the conversation back around to the social and economic condition of Blacks in America. He insisted that we were too complacent about our position. But that didn't mean that he was always stiff and formal. What many people don't know about Malcolm is that he was also a lot of fun. When he decided to let his hair down, watch out! He was incredibly sharp and had a great sense of humor.

Once, when we were sitting in 22 West, a popular restaurant on 135th Street and Fifth Avenue, he told me that this young boxer was coming up from Louisville, Kentucky, to meet him.

"He wants me to instruct him on how to become a Muslim," he said. "But, you know, Hal, it's not that easy. There are a lot of rules to adhere to, a lot of restrictions on what you can and cannot do."

As we spoke, a tour bus pulled up in front of the restaurant. Through the plate-glass windows, I saw a tall, handsome young man step out of the bus and stride toward the door, followed by three or four other people. The young boxer was none other than Cassius Clay.

Now, 22 West is a small restaurant. There is a rounded counter to the right of the front door where patrons can sit and order food. On the left, about a dozen booths line the wall. When Cassius Clay entered, you could feel the excitement. That little place lit up. People didn't know who he was yet, but it didn't matter. All eyes turned to him.

Cassius was charismatic and cocky right from the beginning. He already knew he was the greatest. And he never stopped spouting those little poems and rhymes. But no matter what he said, we took it all in fun. And even when he was joking, there was a certain line that he didn't cross with Malcolm. He was always extremely respectful.

Malcolm demanded respect, and he always got it. But he never hesitated in helping out when he could.

I approached him several times. Once, when a new hospital was being built in Harlem, I discovered that no Black workers were on the construction crews. A group of us decided to picket the site, and I called Malcolm to tell him. I said, "Tomorrow we're supposed to lie down in front of the bulldozers to stop construction at Harlem Hospital until they agree to start hiring Black workers."

Malcolm said, "You know I ain't lying down in front of no bulldozer, Hal. But if anybody hurts you, I'll get involved. I'll be standing across the street in front of the A.M.E. Church with a group of my people."

The next day, we had a group of protesters on the construction site. The crew backed down, and no one was injured, so Malcolm's assistance wasn't necessary, but he and his men were right there in front of the church, waiting and watching, just as he had promised. Malcolm was always there when you needed him, and he never asked for anything in return.

I particularly admired him for his efforts to get addicts off the street and help them stay clean. I didn't agree with his philosophy of getting equal rights by "any means necessary," but I understood that he was actually an asset to the nonviolent movement. We were able to achieve some of our goals simply because our alternative was preferable to Malcolm's in the eyes of the White power structure. The threat was always there, unspoken but clear, that if our demands were not met, the nation would have to deal with Malcolm and the more militant factions.

I participated in a number of civil rights demonstrations in the South during that time, and once got arrested at a sit-in in Chapel Hill, North Carolina, in the late 1950s. Harry Novick was never happy about my involvement in the movement. WLIB walked a thin line in those days, wanting the approval of the NAACP and CORE and the various other civil rights groups but not wanting to alienate advertisers and other supporters of the status quo. But in the same way that Blacks in American society were beginning to demand, and secure, some of the rights that had been denied them, so Black influence was growing in the entertainment business. And nowhere was that influence reflected more than in American music.

The music, however, was coming under attack.

In 1960, Bill Hogan, the Manhattan district attorney, was up for reelection, and I'd heard rumors that his office was conducting an undercover investigation into "commercial bribery" in the music business. His office had dug up some twenty-year-old local statute against accepting favors or money for performing services and was trying to apply this statute to the playing of records on the air. I had never been involved in anything of this kind, so I didn't pay that much attention. Some publishing firms, among them Frank Sinatra's, would send $25 or $50 to every disc jockey in New York as a little thank you if they'd had a good year. I had received some of those thank yous, but that was the only kind of money I had ever received from record publishers.

The investigation by Hogan's office led the management of the various radio stations to prepare affidavits that we all had to sign saying that we had not taken payola. I signed, and so did most of the others. But Alan Freed refused, and in the winter of 1959 he was dropped by both WABC and WNEW-TV. The same thing happened to Mel Leeds, program director at WINS. Leeds went out to Los Angeles, got a job as program director at KDAY, and brought Freed to LA in the spring. I was sorry to see Alan leave New York, but I was astonished when the phone rang one afternoon in May 1960 as I was getting ready to go on the air for my afternoon show. Someone from the district attorney's office told me to get a lawyer because I was about to be charged with commercial bribery.

"For what?" I asked. I was at a total loss.

"Well, for accepting favors and gratuities for playing records," the guy replied.

"You've got to be kidding," I laughed. I couldn't believe he was serious.

"No," he insisted. "You should get a lawyer."

"I don't need a lawyer," I said, and hung up.

A little while later, people from the DA's office showed up at the studio and told me I would have to report to the Elizabeth Street station the next day to be arrested. They assured me that I would be released on my own recognizance. I still didn't take it seriously, and the next day I went to the station unaccompanied by an attorney and unprepared for what I found.

Bill Hogan had decided to milk the occasion for all it was worth, and the entire New York press corps was on hand to record the arraignment of all the major deejays. Alan Freed was there, and so was Peter Tripp, a White deejay who was then with WMGM, Joseph Saccone, who had been the librarian at WMGM, and Mel Leeds, former program director of WINS. Freed and Leeds had flown in from Los Angeles to be arraigned. The two other major Black disc jockeys were there, too—Tommy Smalls of WWRL and Jack Walker, formerly of WOV, who had joined WLIB the previous February. Press photographers lined us all up and took group pictures of us. I was at one end of the line, and when the picture taken by the *Life* photographer ran the following week, I was cropped out of the published print. I complained to the magazine for discriminating against me. At that point, I was still treating the whole matter as a joke.

But it was no joke. The DA's office had investigated this so-called commercial bribery, which was soon dubbed "payola" by the press, going back ten years, and some of the deejays, like Alan Freed, were charged with accepting sums in excess of $200,000 over that period of time. I was charged with thirty-nine counts of taking a total of $9,850 from nine companies.

After the media event was over, I was released on my own recognizance, as promised. I went back to the station, intending to go back on the air. But Harry Novick was waiting for me.

"You know, we're going to have to suspend you until all of this is cleared up," he said.

"For how long?" I asked, incredulous.

"Maybe two or three days," he replied. I did not realize at the time that he was stalling, that he never intended to put me back on the air. I found out later that he had been in contact with Hogan's people for some time and had known exactly what was going to happen. Great and good friend of mine that he pretended to be, he hadn't bothered to warn me. Harry Novick saw the payola scandal as a way to cut me down to size and stop me complaining about the low salaries, small advertising percentages, and poor working conditions that we radio announcers, especially the Blacks in the field, had to suffer. He saw an opportunity to replace me with someone who was less expensive and less powerful.

Harry suspended Jack Walker, too. Over at WWRL, Tommy Smalls was fired outright; and Peter Tripp and Joseph Saccone were suspended by WMGM.

Friends rallied to my defense. The Reverend Oberia Dempsey, head of the Baptist Ministers conference in New York and assistant minister to Adam Clayton Powell Jr. at the Abyssinian Baptist Church, called me and asked what they could do to help.

"I sure would like to get back on the air," I said, and so he offered to call Harry Novick and invite him to meet with a group of ministers. Novick met with the group and told them, "Hal is a big man with the young people. This will set a very bad example for them, a guy like him taking money to play records."

The ministers argued that I had been indicted, not convicted. "This is not a guilty verdict," they said. "You should show your support by letting Hal stay on the job until he is found guilty or not guilty." Harry said only that he would take their recommendation under advisement.

Adam Clayton Powell also offered to talk to Novick on my behalf. But Novick told Adam that he was afraid he might lose his FCC license if he let me go back to work. Adam called the Federal Communications Commission and asked for confirmation of Novack's assertion. The FCC informed Adam the case had nothing to do with them, since it involved a local New York statute, not federal laws. Putting me back on the air was entirely up to the station owners.

Two days after my suspension, I got a phone call from Dave Braithwaite, a Black engineer at WLIB whom I had been instrumental in bringing to the station. Dave told me that Harry was going to put Jack Walker in my place. I had brought Jack Walker to WLIB from WADO. He was also under indictment for accepting payola, but at WADO. Harry's rationalization was that he could put Jack on because his indictment concerned another station. Talk about splitting hairs!

So Jack Walker took over my air time, and I could see that my suspension was going to last a lot longer than Harry had let on.

At first, my allies rallied to my defense. Local ministers whom I had helped with fund-raisers and other efforts formed a special Hal Jackson Committee and organized rallies of support. They set up picket lines outside the station. The signs read, "No Hal Jackson, No WLIB! Turn Off Your Radio!" But Harry Novick was unmoved. As the weeks wore on, the picketing stopped. My phone, which used to ring at all hours of the day or night with calls from people wanting my attention, was silent. I had never felt so alone. For the first time in my life, I was paralyzed with doubt. "How could this be happening to me?" I kept asking myself. I was a pillar of the community. The White House had honored me on three separate occasions for my charitable and humanitarian efforts. How could I suddenly be considered a criminal.

It was my lowest time. On top of the payola indictment, my personal life was a shambles. Julia and I had separated, and she and the girls who were still at home had moved to Lenox Terrace, the priciest address in Harlem. I had an apartment on

Television

who will crash TV gates.

HAL JACKSON, dynamic radio and TV personality.

to a Manhattan physician.

IF THINGS go as planned, some time this Fall, 100 million television viewers across the country may be startled to see glamorous Negro models demonstrating advertised products on television. The models chosen for these choice assignments will receive commissions and salaries ranging from $75 to $125 for a two-minute TV commercial.

In line for these TV jobs are a group of ten attractive Sepia Sirens who are billed as "Hal Jackson's American Beauties". Hal Jackson, a popular radio disc jockey and television emcee, first organized the group nearly a year ago and spent several months training the ten hand-picked glamour gals to walk, talk, and act before television cameras. Then, he sold several large companies and manufacturers the idea of selling their products to Negro televiewers by letting the "American Beauties" merchandise the products on televised shows.

With powerful sponsors backing Hal and his American Beauties, chances are the networks will be forced to break a precedent which has existed since the advent of

television: the unwritten law which up until now has discouraged major networks from employing Negro entertainers or models to work regularly before cameras. Although as of this writing, no major network has ever hired Negro models to merchandise televised products it is almost a certainty that they will begin doing so this Fall primarily because of Hal Jackson's determined efforts toward this goal.

When Hal Jackson first went seeking for sponsors to put his American Beauties on television shows, the sponsors were frankly dubious about the outcome of such a plan.

"White Southern viewers," they argued, "wouldn't stand for such a thing!"

Hal Jackson overcame that barrier by inviting several prospective television sponsors and TV executives to look over his "American Beauties" at a press conference. After the conference was over, one prominent television executive who had watched Hal's Beauties parade before the gathering of bigshots, pulled Hal to one side and whispered to him.

32

Advocates for Black models for network television ads, 1960s

the corner of Lenox Avenue and 135th Street. I was supporting two households, but I had no money coming in. I couldn't
file for unemployment because I had only been suspended, not
fired. I was practically broke, and my spirit was nearly broken
as well.

Adam Clayton Powell was a big help to me at this time—
not as the powerful congressman from Harlem but as a Baptist
minister. In Washington, he was the most powerful Black in
Congress, and for many years, as chairman of the House Labor
and Education Committee, the most powerful Black man in
the country. He was arrogant and charismatic, and he had a lot
of enemies. But I saw him mostly in his capacity as minister to
a large flock of poor people. He would come to town every
weekend to preach at Abyssinian Baptist Church and other-
wise minister to his congregation. I would stop by his office
and sit with him, watching how he took care of the many
people who came to him for aid. Adam cared very deeply
about the homeless and the poor and would do whatever he
could to help them.

Adam saw politics as a way to help people, and knowing
of my own efforts in that area, he once tried to talk me into
running for office. I'd be a shoo-in for the New York State
Assembly, he argued. But I was not interested in a political
career. To my mind, politicians had to compromise too
much.

Sitting in Adam's office and seeing other people with problems helped me put my own in perspective. And Adam helped
me find a renewed faith in God.

"Don't you lose faith, Hal," Adam said to me. "You'll be

back, and you'll be bigger and better than ever. But you must remember that God has control of all things."

After a while, I accepted that God was trying to shake me up, that I had been too wrapped up in my own success and my own importance. It was a humbling experience. But it was also good for me. Without that new understanding, I never would have taken a job cleaning office buildings at night.

I happened to run into a guy who owned a cleaning firm and for whom I had done some radio advertising. He asked how I was doing, and I was truthful about my financial circumstances. He said, "Well, Hal, you know all I have is this cleaning business, but if you want to do some night work, I'll pay you top dollar." So, a few nights later, the former star broadcaster Hal Jackson found himself cleaning New York City office buildings. When I figured out that the cleaning job wasn't bringing in enough money to cover my bills, I took on a second job driving a cab. I wasn't too proud to do honest work for honest pay, and I needed the money. Fortunately, I managed to get back on the air waves. I was able to quit those jobs and move on with my life doing the thing that I loved doing most. Once again, I got back behind the microphone.

*Hal Jackson outside courthouse after being cleared from
the payola scandal, early 1960s*

Dear Mr. Ret

COCA-C

advertising sc

popular "Hou

WLIB.

So be sure

8.

STARTING OVER

Although I understood how serious the "commercial bribery" charges against me were, I didn't have the money for an attorney to represent me. Fortunately, a White attorney named Earl Zaidins contacted me and offered to represent me for a modest fee. He had read enough about the scandal to know that the charges against me were minor compared to those against some of the other deejays. He understood my determination to go to trial and prove my innocence rather than try to settle out of court. He did some digging and found out that the authorities were trying to find witnesses who would testify that I had accepted money to play certain records, offering these potential witnesses immunity from prosecution if they would testify against me. He also found out that, so far, the authorities had come up with nothing.

The legal wheels moved slowly then, just as they do now, and weeks went by when Earl had nothing to report. Confident that he was doing all he could for me. I concentrated on making a living.

While I was under indictment in the payola scandal, I was persona non grata on radio in New York; but in other localities the payola thing wasn't any big deal. Nobody cared about it in Philadelphia. Jocko Henderson lived there. I had helped him establish himself in New York when he arrived there from Baltimore. I had talked Frank Schiffman into letting him host the show at the Apollo Theater for a week, and he was so popular that Morris Levy hired him for WADO. At the time he called me, Jocko was living in Philadelphia, where he had a daily show over WDAS, and traveling to the city for his daily WADO show, which he sometimes taped at his house in Philly. Jocko and another Philadelphia deejay, Georgie Woods, who was also on WDAS but who had worked with me at WLIB in New York, invited me down to Philly to see what could be worked out for me. I even stayed at Georgie's house while they set up a meeting with Bob Klein, who was then running WDAS.

Klein and I talked about me doing a rhythm and blues show over WDAS. He also told me that they were starting an FM station, which was a very new thing at the time, that would be part of the WQXR classical network. Klein wanted to know if I could handle classical music. "I can handle anything," I told him. So I started doing a four-hour classical show over WDAS-FM, from 6 to 10 each morning. Through the WQXR network, it was fed into stations in New York and Delaware, as well as Philadelphia. After that show, I would do a four-hour rhythm and blues show over WDAS-FM. When I went off the air in the afternoon, I would go over to Jocko's house, pick up the

Julia Jackson, Ann Roberts, Hal, and Jewell Jackson, 1961

latest show he had taped for WADO in New York, catch the
4 P.M. train, and deliver the tape to WADO. I did this for about
five months.

Being back on the air waves also gave me a chance to get
back into the live entertainment scene. I did several benefits in
Atlantic City, New Jersey, and when Ray Charles contacted me
about hosting a show at the Coliseum there, I was happy to accept. On the day of the show, I rode down from New York to
Atlantic City on Ray's tour bus with his thirty-piece orchestra.

Ray was due to fly down later in his private plane. We got all set up in the Coliseum, and the audience started to arrive, and pretty soon 8,000 expectant fans were jammed into the place, which was supposed to hold 5,000.

Showtime came, and there was still no Ray Charles. So I got up and introduced the band and the opening act. Then we got word that Ray was fogged in at the airport but would get there as soon as he could. The band kept playing—for three hours. Meanwhile, the fans started getting restless. There was considerable drinking going on; people were angry and demanding their money back. There was exactly one exit, and I was worried that if people started trying to leave en masse it would be a disaster. Fights were breaking out by the time I took charge, organizing a "community sing" and an impromptu talent show. Ray finally arrived more than four hours late, having spent three hours on a bus, but I'd kept his audience for him. The *Philadelphia Tribune* carried a front-page article the following week:

ANGRY FANS RIOT AS RAY CHARLES SHOWS UP FOUR HOURS LATE

Atlantic City Police Have Busy Day Calming 8,000 Jammed in Coliseum Seating 5,000

Atlantic City—Blind blues singer arrived more than four hours late for a scheduled appearance early Tuesday morning at a

☆ *Cerebral Palsy Telethon poster child with
Brooke Shields and Hal, 1970s*

☆ *Hal, Lena Horne, and her manager Sherman Sneed at the* **CANDACE AWARDS** *at the Waldorf Astoria, 1980s*

☆ *Stevie Wonder, Debi Jackson, and Hal chat after an interview on* **SUNDAY MORNING CLASSICS,** *1980s*

☆ *Tina Turner and Hal, 1980s*

☆ *Hal and Bob Marley, 1980s*

☆ *Promotional poster for* DREAMGIRLS *starring Deborah Burrell, Sheryl Lee Ralph (a former Talented Teen) and Loretta Devine, early 1980s*

☆ *Don King, Hal, and Marvin Gaye at Radio City*
Music Hall concert sponsored by King, 1982

☆ *Hal, Nancy Wilson, and Debi Jackson, 1983*

☆ Hal and Don Cornelious with 1984's Hal Jackson's
Talented Teen International contest winner, Michelle Thomas

☆ Herbie Hancock, Miss America Suzette Charles,
Quincy Jones, and Hal at the Sony Innovators Awards, 1984

☆ *Berry Gordy and Hal, 1985*

☆ *Gracie Mansion reception for* LISTEN UP, *a film
about the life of Quincy Jones. Hal is pictured with
Gerald Busby, Clarence Avant, and Quincy Jones, 1986*

☆ *"The House Where Jack Was Born," in Charleston,
South Carolina, 1987*

☆ *Hal with 1987's Hal Jackson's Talented Teen International*
contest winner, Tammy Townsend, and Don Cornelius at
an appearance on **SOUL TRAIN,** *1987*

☆ **LL COOL J,** *1988's Hal Jackson's Talented Teen*
International contest winner, Kiya Winston, Hal, and
JET T.V. *co-host Debra Crabble, 1988*

☆ Jocko Henderson, Billy Erskine, Dave Clark, Hal, and
Jack the Rapper at Impact Radio Convention, 1989

☆ Hal with Mayor Ed Koch at City Hall celebrating
Hal's fiftieth anniversary on radio, 1989

 Hal with Mariah Carey and Debi at the
Sony Club Listening Party, late 1980s

☆ *Hal and Jewell Jackson McCabe at the Apollo Wall of Fame, 1989*

☆ *Hal with Bill Cosby and the Reverend Jesse Jackson during* **NAACP** *radiothon, 1990s*

☆ *Aretha Franklin, Hal, and Clive Davis at*
Arista Records party, 1990s

☆ BOYZ II MEN *and Hal with 1991's Hal Jackson's Talented*
Teen contest winner, Myisha Richmond, 1991

☆ *Congressman Charles Rangel with Hal, 1991*

☆ *Hal with Hal Jackson's Talented Teen International*
contestants greeted by Mayor David Dinkins at
City Hall, 1991

☆ Denzel Washington with Hal, 1990s

☆ *Hal with Ed Bradley, 1990s*

☆ *Hal with* LL COOL J, *1990s*

Cabaret and Dawn dance being staged at Atlantic City's huge Coliseum. More than 8,000 screaming fans, packed into the hall which normally accommodates 5,000, hurled chairs and bottles and engaged in several bloody fights after learning that Charles had not arrived. . . .

Dee Jay Saves Day
Only the quick thinking of Philadelphia disc jockey Hal Jackson prevented a full-scale riot. Jackson, who emceed the affair, organized an impromptu band and then urged the fans to participate in a "community sing." While dance hall police roamed the ballroom breaking up fights, Jackson led the audience in a three-hour songfest as the band played popular rock and roll tunes.

I was regarded as something of a hero after that incident, but I was really just doing my job.

Not long after that near-riot in Atlantic City, I finally had my day in court over the payola scandal. Called to appear one morning at 10 o'clock, Earl Zaidins and I walked in prepared to fight the charges against me. Then the prosecuting attorney stood up and addressed the judge: "We would like to dismiss the charges of commercial bribery against Hal Jackson," he said. That was it, as far as he was concerned. The DA's office had been unable to prove that I had taken payola. They had bigger fish to fry.

But that was not it for me. I was frustrated and furious. I stood up and demanded to know, "What about these last nine months of my life? What about my lost income? Nine months ago you had me on the front page of *The New York Times*. Your apology will probably appear on page 46. Who's going to read that?"

I wanted to sue somebody. I thought of suing the City of New York, but I was told I couldn't do that. Earl had found out that Harry Novick had conspired with the DA's office to bring charges against me, so I sued Novick for $1 million for defamation of character. I organized my own publicity campaign to announce that the charges against me had been dropped.

Everyone else charged in the payola scandal eventually pleaded guilty and received suspended sentences. The scandal finally died down; but it had caused enough of a stir to have national consequences. There were Congressional hearings into the practice of payola, and later a federal law was passed barring commercial bribery.

The radio industry's solution to the payola problem was to create the Top 40 format, which basically gave management control over the play lists of records to be aired on their stations. Before, the play lists had been determined by individual deejays. This change meant that the era of personality radio was over—at least for a time. A number of deejays, White and Black, managed to survive and prosper, but overall, the decade of the 1960s was not a good one for Black radio. Five soul-radio chains (all of them White-owned and managed) rose to dominate twenty stations in key urban markets with large African-American populations, including New York, Chicago, Memphis, and Washington, D.C. They had standardized Top 40 formats, which limited the independence of the Black deejays they employed, and they eliminated most of the local African-American news and public affairs offerings. There was little anyone could do, as long as Whites controlled Black radio.

Not long after the payola charges against me were dropped, I got a call from Fred Barr and Edith Dick, who ran station WWRL in Queens, New York. It was a small station at the top of the dial, with a weak signal. It had some foreign-language programming and a lot of gospel music. It also had one R&B show, which Fred and Edith wanted me to take over.

I wanted to get back on the New York air waves, and although going to WWRL was like starting at the bottom again, I decided it was worth a try. WWRL organized a big publicity campaign to announce my arrival—"Hal Jackson is back and WWRL has got him"—and the Baptist Ministers Conference gave me a surprise welcome-home party. I was glad to be back.

I wasted no time trying to build up the audience for WWRL. I found out about a gadget that could enhance the station's weak signal. Called a "stay level," it could be installed in the transmitter to push the signal out. So I got one for WWRL, and people were able to hear us all over New York and even into New Jersey. This helped us attract more advertisers and made the station more attractive to potential investors. After I had been with WWRL about a year, a man named Egmont

Sonderling contacted me. He was interested in buying the station, getting rid of the foreign-language programming, and aiming all its programming at the Black market. He wanted to know if I would stay on and continue my regular program, plus take the job as program director and line up the talent needed to appeal to a Black audience. I agreed, and when he took over the station he put me in charge of all the programming.

As soon as word got out about the new programming direction, I started hearing from a lot of Black deejays. I hired Enoch Gregory, who had been with WWRL as a newscaster earlier but who had then moved on to join Al Lamphian at WNJR and then gone to Chicago. Bill McCreary had been a newscaster, but I brought him on to do a jazz show. I contacted him through Alma John, who was doing a women's program on WWRL. My biggest coup was getting Rocky G. He was a fine announcer for WLIB, but what really made me happy was taking him away from Harry Novick.

I have never worked harder in my life than I did building up WWRL. I used all the tricks of the trade that I had learned from my years in broadcasting. One of the sponsors of my daily show was the Tip-Top Baking Company, and I had the idea of Tip-Top cosponsoring a talent contest on my daily show. Hundreds of talented amateurs clamored to appear on my show, competing for a first prize that included a recording contract and a one-week appearance at the Apollo Theater. I did live remotes from stores that sold Tip-Top bread—one store sold 510 loaves of bread in three and a half hours—and I even gave pep talks to the bread route salesmen. I had a great partnership with the Tip-Top Baking Company. It sold a lot of their product, in-

Smokey Robinson and the Miracles with Hal at
Palisades Amusement Park, 1960s

creased the audience for WWRL, and gave a lot of bright youngsters a chance to show their talents on the air.

During the Christmas season of 1961 I sponsored another holiday drive for the needy. We set up a collection point in Harlem, and people brought money, clothing, and toys. We collected enough money to buy truckloads of chicken, cabbage, yams, white potatoes, sugar, canned peaches, salt pork, oranges, apples, and candy. Hundreds of volunteers packed 1,000 baskets of food for distribution. A moving company volunteered the use of its fleet of vans to take the food and other goods to five distribution points throughout the metropolitan area. That particular Christmas drive stands out from among the many I have organized over the years, because it proved that I still had the support of the people of New York.

By 1962, I was back to doing twenty things at a time. In addition to my regular show and my program manager duties on WWRL, and my work for various charities, I was cohosting concerts in Central Park with Ron Delsener, sponsored by Schaeffer beer. That year, I also started doing live broadcasts from Freedom Land, an amusement park in the Bronx that operated in the summertime. The park had a theater-in-the-round, and I did my remotes from there attracting new audiences and bigger receipts at the gate. Word of this success reached Mrs. Irving Rosenthal (who was a songwriter under her maiden name, Gladys Shelley), and she visited Freedom Land to see what I was doing. She and her husband owned Palisades Amusement Park on the New Jersey side of the Hudson River, and soon afterward, I received an offer to become the official host of Palisades Park.

It was a good business decision on the Rosenthals part to bring me on. I had a following and could attract more Black patrons to the amusement park, which had a very low Black attendance. On the other hand, I was known as a general-audience personality, so I wouldn't scare the White patrons away. Through my concerts in Central Park sponsored by Schaeffer, I had access to a lot of the top acts that the Rosenthals were interested in booking for their stage.

I had one major reservation about accepting the Rosenthals' offer. Although the rides at the park were open to all, the pool, advertised as "the world's largest salt-water swimming

Promotional billboard for concerts at
Palisades Amusement Park, 1960s

New Jersey State officials including the Payne brothers and Hal with the Supremes' Florence Ballard, Mary Wilson, and Diana Ross, 1960s

pool" was segregated. To use it, you had to belong to a club, and the club was open to Whites only. But I looked at the exposure being host at the park would give me. I would do all the park's radio and TV commercials, which amounted to seventy or eighty a day during the summer season, and my face would be on billboards. I also figured I would find a way to change that Whites-only pool policy from the inside.

Until the Palisades Amusement Park closed its gates in 1970, I served as the official host and announcer. "Come on over to the Palisades!" was my slogan, and it and my face became synonymous with the park. A British comic book even featured me in a segment about Palisades Park. I did remotes from the park on weekends, playing records and interviewing artists. I hosted and produced the big star-studded shows that were presented free on Saturday and Sunday afternoons, and I brought in many of the top acts of the era. White acts I brought in included the Rolling Stones, Paul Anka, and Bobby Vinton.

By this time, Berry Gordy had changed the name of his record company from Hitsville, USA to Motown and had his first big bits. Both he and the kids he groomed had worked hard for their success. When he first started touring his acts, Berry was with them all the way. I once saw Berry stick with the Supremes doing twenty-one nights at the Copacabana, two shows a night, go straight from there to the Catskills for another ten days of show, and then on to Atlantic City. He made the Supremes a national institution and Diana Ross a superstar. I featured all the great Motown acts on my shows, including the Supremes, the Temptations, Gladys Knight and the Pips, the Four Tops, and Stevie Wonder.

I hadn't been the official host at Palisades Amusement Park long before I asked the Rosenthals if I could bring in some poor children on weekdays, when the park was not crowded (the big crowds came on the weekends). Seeing this program as a chance to show that they were community service–minded, the Rosenthals gave me the go-ahead, and I started bringing in busloads of poor children, Black and White, two times a week. The kids got to go on all the rides for free, and before management realized what had happened, they were all over the pool.

Hal during promotional stop with Althea Gibson
for Mr. Big Bread, 1960s

I became especially close to one young guest. Betty Robinson was about 12 when we first met. She lived on West 114th Street and came from a family of fourteen children. She came over to the Palisades on a bus filled with kids from Harlem one day, and she just stood out for her energy and pep. She kind of attached herself to me and followed me around the park, and it was only after a while that I realized she was blind. When it was time to return to the bus, she asked if she could come back again the next week. Normally, we brought in different children each time, but something about Betty was so special that I made an exception for her and arranged for her to visit quite often. I got to know Betty and her family, who were quite poor, and I would help them out whenever I could. Betty's dream was to become a secretary; I got her a typewriter and arranged for her to have a special typing course. After she graduated from high school at the special school for the blind that she attended, I arranged for Betty to get a seeing-eye dog and to spend eight weeks in New Jersey learning how to handle him. Betty realized her dream of becoming a secretary. And later, she married a sighted man and had three children. We still keep in touch.

I received my fourth presidential commendation for my work with young people—for both the antidrug programs and the special outings for poor kids I arranged at Palisades Amusement Park. President John F. Kennedy honored me at a special luncheon at the White House and, at one point, pulled me aside and asked me how my antidrug programs could be applied on a national scale.

During the early 1960s I received many honors. In 1964, I celebrated my twenty-fifth year in broadcasting. It was back in 1939 that I had first gone on the air with *The Bronze Review* over WINX in Washington, D.C. Twenty-six New York area or-

Disabled children enjoy a moment with Hal, 1960s

ganizations sponsored a testimonial dinner. I was also voted Disc Jockey of the Year for my community and charitable work. The awards ceremony was held at the Metro Goldwyn Meyer studios in Hollywood, and Richard Chamberlain (who was at the height of his popularity as TV's Dr. Kildare) presented the award.

But by this time in my life I should have realized that when you are riding high, people get jealous and try to bring you down. One day without warning, Frank Ward, the general manager of WWRL, who was a racist and a heavy drinker to boot, came to me with an ultimatum from the station's management: if 1 wanted to remain on the air, I would have to give up my work at Palisades Amusement Park. He said that the other WWRL deejays were complaining that they weren't getting the same opportunities for publicity and promotional income.

I immediately told Ward that the agreement was between Palisades and me, not him or the WWRL management. The exchange got very heated, and finally he ended it by saying, "Just make up your mind. Either everyone goes to Palisades or you won't go back."

"Oh, yes I will," I said as I stormed out of his office.

But then I started thinking, and I doubted Ward's explanation of why he had asked me to drop a major gig. I suspected that the station management was worried that I was getting too big for them to control. I went to see Malcolm X that night and

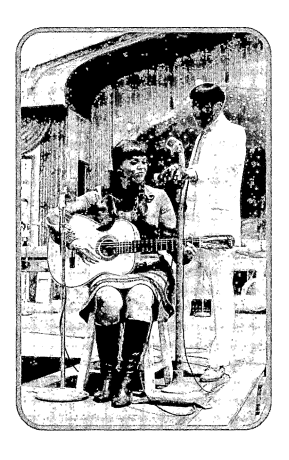

Linda Ronstadt with Hal at Palisades Amusement Park, late 1960s

told him what had happened. Malcolm offered to help me with a public show of support. But, by then I had calmed down, analyzed my situation, and realized that I could act from a position of strength. I had big national advertisers—Budweiser, Schaeffer, Pepsi-Cola—who would go with me to whatever station I worked for. So the following day I called a press conference and announced that I was leaving WWRL. Then I disappeared for 48 hours.

I drove over to Palisades Amusement Park and told Irving Rosenthal what I had done. He told me not to worry. "Let's go

Hal with the Temptations at
Palisades Amusement Park, late 1960s

to a different station," he said. "We'll guarantee that you'll broadcast from the park." I spent the night with the Rosenthals at their house on Fifth Avenue.

The management of WWRL was surprised and dismayed. Their blackmail attempt had backfired. There were frantic calls from Egdemont Sonderling's office, begging me not to leave. But I had made my announcement, and I was through with WWRL.

It was a time in my life when I was starting over in more ways than one. After being separated for a number of years, Julia and I were finally divorced.

9.

WITH KINGS AND QUEENS

hrough Al Lamphian, I had become friends with Len Mirelson, the general manager of WNJR over in Union, New Jersey. I called Len and told him I was available and could bring with me guaranteed advertising revenue plus the Palisades Amusement Park. Len jumped at the chance to hire me and offered me my own show as well as the position of assistant general manager at the station.

It wasn't long after I started working in New Jersey that I got involved in community causes there. I made a lot of appearances in the local high schools, urging the kids to stay off drugs and stay out of trouble. Newark had exploded in a series of riots in the summer of 1964, and I organized a series of concerts for young people to "keep Newark cool."

On several occasions, I accompanied Martin Luther King Jr. on his visits to local schools. On one occasion, we passed a little girl sitting on the front steps, crying her heart out. Dr. King stopped to talk to her.

"Why are you crying?" he asked. "You are Black, and you are beautiful." There were a lot of newspaper reporters around when it happened, and some of them picked up on the exchange. Eventually, the expression became a widely used slogan—Black and beautiful.

I remained involved in the civil rights movement during the 1960s participating in many of the now-historic events of the era. I was at the demonstration in Birmingham, Alabama, in 1962, when Sheriff Bull Connor set dogs and fire hoses on the demonstrators. And I heard Martin's fantastic "I Have a Dream" speech at the 1963 March on Washington. There was such a feeling of togetherness and purpose as marchers, myself included, boarded the thousands of buses that converged on the capital that day. Standing in a holding area behind the Lincoln Memorial, I heard Martin's every word booming from the speakers on the platform.

I also participated in the Selma-to-Montgomery march in 1965 and organized numerous fund-raisers for the SCLC. They were usually star-studded affairs. Martin often stayed with Harry Belafonte when he came to New York, and, when the affairs were at Harry's home, they often featured superstar guests like Sidney Poitier.

Whenever he came to New York, Martin and I tried to meet—usually at our old haunt 22 West, where we would have dinner and get caught up on the latest news.

Martin definitely had premonitions of his own death. The very last time I saw him was a few weeks before he was assassinated. He had been appearing in New Jersey and asked me to

Jane, Hal, and Jewell Jackson, early 1960s

ride to the airport with him. I noticed he was very quiet during the trip, and I asked him what was wrong.

"I just feel I'll never see all this beauty and all these people again," he said.

"Oh, come on, Rev.," I said. "What are you talking about?"

"I'm going to Memphis next week to help the sanitation men in their fight. I've got more heavy plans, and life is going to be very busy. I don't think I'll be back here."

On April 4, 1968, I was hosting one of those "keep Newark cool" concerts. Lots of stars had volunteered to perform, and we had a great crowd. The Newark police were out in force outside the school and were pushing the kids around. and I went out to talk to the cops and asked them to please take it easy. They warned me that the place was overcrowded, and I told them, "Well, then, I'd better get back inside and get the show underway." I went out on the stage and asked everybody to be quiet and orderly, so the police would have no cause to interfere, and then I introduced the opening act.

About midway through the show, a young girl came to me and whispered, "Mr. Jackson, I was just in the ladies' room, and there's a radio on and somebody said Dr. King was shot."

"Oh, no!" I exclaimed. "Well, don't say anything about it right now."

She agreed to keep the news to herself, and I looked out at all those young people in the audience and wondered how I was going to get through the show.

About an hour later, just before the show was scheduled to end, one of the performers stepped up to the microphone and announced that Dr. King was dead, shot down in Memphis. There was a shocked silence, then kids started yelling and crying. I knew I had to control this crowd, so I took the mike and asked everyone to stay seated.

"Stay calm and let's do what Dr. King would want us to do," I said. "Please don't rush outside and start raising the devil. That's just what the police are waiting for. I'm going out first, and I'm going to be out there when you come out."

All over the nation, communities were going up in flames, as people expressed their grief and frustration. But the whole audience at my concert left quietly and dispersed in an orderly fashion.

As I drove back to New York that night, I heard on the radio that people in Harlem were going berserk, and from the window of my apartment at Lenox Avenue and 135th Street I could see fires and hear shouts. The whole thing was so crazy, because the rioters weren't hurting anyone but

Promotor Ron Delsener, Mayor John Lindsay, and Hal introduce the Schaeffer Central Park Concert Series, late 1960s

themselves and their own communities. All those fires and looting meant businesses and jobs that wouldn't be there anymore. But I could also appreciate the anger and frustration. Still, burned-out buildings were not a fitting memorial to Dr. King's memory. I thought his birthday should be a national holiday.

I started talking up the idea the next morning on my radio show and continued promoting it for a year and a half on and off the air. I asked my listeners to send me a letter supporting the cause, and at the end of eighteen months I was able to deliver 700,000 letters to Representatives Shirley Chisholm and John Conyers, who introduced the first bill in Congress calling for the holiday to honor Dr. King. It took another thirteen years or so before the dream became a reality, but by that time so many influential people were in favor of the idea that the movement had acquired a life of its own. The White House Rose Garden wasn't large enough to hold everyone who had worked for the passage of the bill when President Reagan finally signed it into law in 1983.

In 1968, the same year Dr. King was assassinated, I had the opportunity to host *Frontiers of Faith*, a Sunday show on the NBC network. I was the first Black host ever to appear on that show, and I hoped it would lead to more work in television, a medium I really wanted to get more involved in. That same year I developed a television show that I hoped to build into a series. It was called *Clown Town*, based on a song by Gladys Shelley, and was filmed entirely on location at Palisades Amusement Park. It was a great show, featuring Bobby Vinton and Odetta. Unfortunately, shooting disrupted the business of the park, and Irving Rosenthal decided he didn't want that. I had financed and produced the show myself and had to settle for airing it on WPIX and a few other stations as a one-time event. But I had much better luck with a teenage talent pageant that I got involved in the following year.

Since my separation from Julia, another woman had become increasingly important in my life. Alice LaBrie Hille and her husband had been friends for many years. After her husband was killed in an automobile accident in the early 1960s, Alice was alone with her baby son, Gerald, and our relationship gradually deepened. On March 7, 1969, we were married in Las Vegas.

Alice worked for the television production company of Goodson Todman; but she did a lot of independent producing on the side. She was assistant producer of the TV show *Soul*, hosted by Ellis Haizlip. She knew the TV production business, and soon we would be involved in a business partnership as well as in life.

In 1969, the same year Alice and I got married, I was director for special events and concerts at Madison Square Garden's Felt Forum. Al Cooperman, chief operating officer of the Garden, asked if I would host the Miss Black America pageant scheduled for the Garden in August. The first Miss Black America had been crowned the previous year in Atlantic City, but the pageant was going to be held in New York from then on. The pageant would be televised in syndication across the United States and even overseas—a first for a Black entertainment show. It would be produced by none other than Alice

LaBrie Hille. I didn't hesitate to say yes. I had never worked with Alice professionally, but I knew she would be great to work with, and she was.

The main reason behind the Miss Black America pageant, of course, was the lily-white nature of the Miss America contest. No Black woman had ever made it to the finals of the Miss America pageant, and I doubt if they were even in the local competition. The Miss Black America contest aimed to show that Black is beautiful, and the contestants proved the point. There were seventeen contestants in that 1969 pageant, which was not bad, considering that it was only the second such contest and the girls' travel and lodging expenses, clothing, etc., had to be sponsored by local businesses or organizations.

Alice and I worked hard to line up professional talent so the program would be a real showcase for Black entertainment as well. Stevie Wonder was the headliner—he was still Little Stevie Wonder then—and in addition we had the Impressions and the Reverend James Cleveland and the Cleveland Singers, a gospel group.

Berry Gordy called and suggested we put a new group, the Jackson Five, on the show. Berry had just discovered them, and they had never been on television. I saw the Miss Black America contest as a chance to showcase them. They were a playful bunch, jumping all over each other and roughhousing—all except Michael. Even then he was shy and soft-spoken. So many of the people around him seemed to be pulling him in different directions, and he tried to please them all at the same time. He seemed so fragile that I wondered whether he would be all right out there onstage. But the second he stepped into the spotlight, he lit up and became absolutely dynamic. No one could touch him. When the show was over, all that creative energy just kind of disappeared, and he was a shy little boy once again.

The pageant was the Jackson Five's first performance in New York as well as their television debut, and their performance proved beyond a doubt that they were destined for stardom. Years later, in the late 1980s I believe, I was at a Michael Jackson concert when he saw me and pulled me aside. "You gave us our first TV break," he said, "I never forgot."

The following year, the Miss Black America contest was again held in New York, and Alice and I repeated our roles in it. This time there were thirty-one contestants, so the contest was growing. There was clearly a need for such contests for young Black women. After that second Miss Black America pageant, Alice and I came up with the idea for a contest for youngsters ages 13 to 16—Miss Black Teenage America. We intended to emphasize talent; we saw it as a way to showcase the talented Black youngsters across the nation.

Alice had lots of contacts with the Black sororities, especially the Deltas, and through them and other interested organizations and individuals we set up a system of state talent contests whose winners would get to participate in a national televised competition. While Alice was busy lining up sponsors and getting the state preliminaries underway, I searched for a financial backer for the national contest, which we had decided to hold in Atlanta, Georgia. By then, Atlanta was emerging as a symbol of the New South and had a Black assistant mayor, Maynard Jackson (who later served two separate terms as mayor); in addition, we knew that production costs would be lower than in New York.

We had tremendous response to the contest idea, and throughout the late spring and early summer of 1971 there were local Miss Black Teenage America contests. The finals were scheduled for July 28. Then, two months before that date, the company that had promised to underwrite the expenses for the finals went bankrupt!

We could have canceled the finals, but we knew the heartbreak that this would cause all the talented youngsters who were waiting for their big moments—not to mention all the organizations and individuals who had seen to it that the young women had gotten this far. So, out of necessity, one of the first Black production companies in the country, Hal Jackson Productions, was born. I was executive producer, and Alice was producer and writer. In actuality, Alice was the one who set the whole thing up; it would not have come into existence without her. The show went on as scheduled on July 28, 1971, but not without one more minor hitch.

A couple from Danville, Virginia, the Charitys, were planning their own Miss Black Teenage America pageant for September, and they went to court in New York to try to prevent our show from going on. We were able to present evidence in court that we had been planning the event for months, and the Charitys withdrew their case.

We didn't have time to worry about syndication at that late date, so we put the show on and taped it, deciding to worry about syndicating it later. It was a great show, with special guest appearances by Ronny Dyson and Howard Rice of *Room 222*, a popular 1970s television program. June Kelly of Fort Worth, Texas, was our first winner; she later went on to study medicine at Meharry Medical College.

We wanted to continue the program, but we knew we couldn't do that without getting the word out, and the way to do that was to get the program on syndicated television. Alice edited the show into a 90-minute format, and I got in touch with some of my loyal sponsors to purchase commercial spots for the show, so we could tell the local stations we approached that the show was partially sponsored already. Fortunately, my faithful sponsor from the past, Pepsi-Cola, agreed to partial sponsorship. The remaining spots could be sold to local advertisers by the individual stations.

Alice and I had never been involved in the business of syndication, but we had no choice. Alice was especially good at pitching the Miss Black Teenage America pageant as an important show for Black people to see. But the main reason we succeeded in selling the show was that FCC requirements had been put in place that mandated a certain percentage of shows for minority audiences in areas of substantial minority populations. We managed to get the show aired in some twenty-five markets, including some of the top markets in the nation and some network-owned and operated stations.

The Miss Black Teenage America pageant was being broadcast across the country when the Charitys (the couple from Danville, Virginia) held their Black Teenage America

Hal and Michael Jackson with Sheryl Pillard, 1978 winner of
Hal Jackson's Talented Teen International contest

pageant in Baltimore in September, forcing Alice and me to
go to court to protect our right to the name of the pageant.
It was really just a nuisance case, but it was important to us
that our pageant not be discredited and the public confused.
We had the documents to prove that we had filed our first-
use date with the U.S. Department of Patents a full year before the Charitys had, and we succeeded in enjoining them
from usurping our trademark.

A few years later, we changed the name of the pageant
from Miss Black Teenage America to Hal Jackson's Talented
Teens International. We didn't want to deal with discrimination suits from White teenagers, but we also wanted to stress
the talent aspect of the competition. The contest became

very popular in the Caribbean nations, where the population is multiracial and where it didn't make sense to try to enforce artificial barriers around color. The winner of the 1982 contest was Kristel Henderson of the U.S. Virgin Islands. Alice and I tried to start a similar boys' contest one year, but we didn't get anywhere with it. At that age, boys are more interested in being in groups, not displaying their talents as individuals.

The contest became an institution in the Black community and, by 1982, had expanded to thirty-seven states, territories, and independent nations. Although we had planned in the beginning to hold it in a different place each year, we found that we could get the necessary backing only in the major entertainment centers, so more often than not it was held in either New York or Los Angeles. The 1982 contest was held at the John F. Kennedy Center for the Performing Arts in Washington, D.C. It took a lot of work to line up sponsors, not only for the finals but also for the local contests. The pageant also cost a lot of money, some of which was defrayed by syndication revenues. Each contestant received ten weeks of training in their particular talent or skill. The girls competed for scholarships and cash prizes, and the highlight of each top winner's reign was an all-expense-paid trip to the U.S. Virgin Islands.

The fact that we focused on talent helped us get the backing of the entertainment business, especially the record companies, and of individual entertainers. One year Harry Belafonte treated all the finalists to an after-theater party at the Greek Theater in Los Angeles and talked to each girl individually. In 1976, all the finalists were treated to a trip to the U.S. Virgin Islands, and Sidney Poitier spent three hours with them at the airport. All the guest artists who have worked the final competition show have been patient and supportive of the girls.

The Talented Teens International Scholarship Competition is now more than three decades old, and it has helped hundreds of girls. Most of the winners have not gone on to careers in the entertainment field, though Tai Jimenez of New York City, who won the contest in 1985, went on to join the Dance Theater of Harlem as one of its principal dancers and Jada Pinkett is an actress and married to Will Smith.

I don't mean to ignore the individuals and organizations who worked so hard on the local level; it took all of them to make the contest a success. I had met my current wife, Debi, fifteen years before we married, when she started doing volunteer work for the contest. Deborah Bolling got involved in the contest at the urging of a family friend, who thought it might help her advance her career. From the beginning, I was impressed by her creative ability and jubilant spirit. Her youthful "Peter Pan" attitude mirrored the enthusiasm that inspired Hal Jackson's Talented Teens International from the beginning.

Debi approached her volunteer tasks with a dedication to my vision that caught my attention. Our relationship grew over the years and evolved into marriage in 1987, after Alice and I parted ways. I always encouraged Debi's career, and through hard work and sheer determination she, too, has become a recognized voice on the air. Known as "Debi

B.," she can be heard along with me on WBLS's *Sunday Morning Classics*. She does voice-overs and promotional ads for several consumer products and has developed into a unique talent with a real future in broadcasting.

I've gotten ahead of myself talking about the Talented Teens International, but providing such great opportunities to so many talented youngsters is one of the proudest accomplishments of my life. Still, even as the Talented Teen contests were evolving, other opportunities were opening up for me.

"The devil didn't make me do this—Best wishes, Hal."

Flip Wilson

●

"The Pips and I join in expressing our gratitude for your friendship over the years."

Gladys Knight

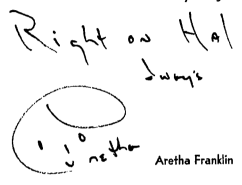

Aretha Franklin

"Best of luck in your future endeavors."

Earl Monroe

●

"Hal Jackson, is one heck of a beautiful person. A warm guy who has helped a lot of people get started: including Percy Sutton."

Percy Sutton
Borough President, Manhattan

●

"Hal Jackson should be commended for his unselfish efforts to bring to the attention of countless thousands the importance of being Black . . ."

Eddie O'Jay

"It's nice to be important, but it's important to be nice."

The Osmond Family

●

"I'm so very appreciative of the fact that Hal Jackson continues to give me credit for bringing him to New York. Because of his enormous success this makes me look so good that I must now tell the truth . . . I was paid to get him out of Washington."

Billy Rowe

●

"I first met Hal Jackson over 20 years ago. Ageless Hal, is the same wonderful guy today that he was then. Perhaps his secret is that he is unaffected by adversity or success and treats those two imposters just the same."

David Dinkins

●

"HAL JACKSON has a deep understanding of human needs. The world is improved because Hal Jackson is part of it. I call him 'Mr. Warm, Sincere and Wonderful.' "

Joe Franklin

●

"If it wasn't for guys like Hal Jackson, guys like me wouldn't be."

Al Gee

10.

RADIO STATION OWNER

*I*n 1968, the disc jockeys at WNJR went on strike for better wages. I had maintained my involvement in AFTRA and, at various times, had been elected to offices in the New York local and had served on the national board. I was happy at WNJR, but I had to support the union, so I joined the protest.

The strike was a long one. I remember we started picketing in July in our shirtsleeves, burning up in the summer sun; we were still out picketing on Union Avenue when the snow was coming down in December. In addition to the hardships caused by the weather, we had to watch out for passing cars. There were no sidewalks around the station, and some motorists tried to run us off the road.

I never went back on the air over WNJR. Instead, Pepsi-Cola offered to bring me back to New York. The company would sponsor me as an independent contractor, so I would be working for Pepsi no matter what station I was on. Ironically, Pepsi wound up buying air time on

WLIB, whose owner, Harry Novick, I was suing for $1 million.

Harry was a smart businessman and was willing to have me back on his airwaves, which now included both AM and FM frequencies, in exchange for Pepsi's money. He also liked the idea of airing my remotes from the Palisades on weekends. The deal we worked out was for me to do the one-hour Pepsi show on weekdays, plus the Palisades remotes. As soon as I agreed to that, Harry offered me another segment of the programming on condition that I drop my suit against him. At that point, I was ready to forget the past and go on, so I consented. Not long afterward, I bought the station.

Actually, I was part of a group of Black investors put together by Percy Sutton, who at the time was president of the Borough of Manhattan. Percy was from San Antonio, Texas, and as I mentioned earlier, had been one of the Tuskegee Flyers during World War II. After the war, he had attended Brooklyn Law School under the GI Bill. The Korean conflict had broken out by then, and Percy returned to the air force, where he served as an intelligence officer and, because of his legal training, as a trial judge advocate.

Returning to New York City, in 1953 Percy opened a law partnership in Harlem with his brother, Oliver, and George Covington. Their clients included Malcolm X and the Baptist Ministers Conference of Greater New York. The firm also worked on several civil rights cases with the NAACP, and Percy served as president of the New York City branch of the NAACP in 1961 and 1962. That's how I got to know him.

Meanwhile, Percy had been trying unsuccessfully to win

local public office. In 1963, he and Charles Rangel, who at the time was also a practicing attorney, formed the John F. Kennedy Democratic Club, which was later renamed the Martin Luther King Jr. Club. With that club as a base, Percy was successful in winning election to the New York State Assembly in 1964 and 1966. (Charles Rangel also won a seat in the state Assembly in 1966 and went on to defeat Adam Clayton Powell Jr. for Harlem's Congressional seat in 1972.)

In 1966, after Manhattan borough president Constance Baker Motley accepted an appointment as a federal judge, the New York City Council nominated Percy to finish Motley's term. Percy was elected to a full term later that year, and was reelected in 1969 and 1973.

Percy Sutton was a smart businessman, and he saw the potential for Black-owned media enterprises. He had already bought *The Amsterdam News* (which he sold in 1975) when he approached me about buying WLIB. Harry Novick was getting a lot of flack about profiting from the Black community without giving much in return, and when Percy contacted him, he was willing to talk terms.

Percy said to me, "Hal, you've made a lot of people rich at all these stations, including Harry Novick. Why don't you team up with me and some other people so you can own something for a change?" That sounded good to me.

The idea of Blacks owning a radio station was not out of the realm of possibility. After all, Jesse B. Layton had bought WERD back in 1949 (which was sold to Whites in 1969 and changed to WXAP), and there were Black-owned stations in Kansas City, Missouri, and Detroit, Michigan. But by the

1970s, radio stations—even those that broadcast in the day-time only—had gotten very pricey, and the average Black person did not have the money to buy them. Both Percy Sutton and Clarence Jones, publisher of *The Amsterdam News*, had approached Harry Novick independently about buying WLIB; but Harry was asking $1.9 million, and that was a lot of money, so Percy and Clarence decided to organize a group of investors to raise enough equity capital to secure the necessary bank financing.

I made a commitment of $20,000, and I was one of the major stockholders. Others included Percy's brother, Oliver; Percy's assistant, Bill Tatum, who would later become the publisher of *The Amsterdam News*; the future mayor of New York, David Dinkins; the singer Roberta Flack; the jazz pianist Billy Taylor; Doc Watkins, a prominent podiatrist; Muriel Petrioni, a gynecologist, and her son, Mal Woolfolk; Jesse Jackson in Chicago; and Carl McCall, who would later become comptroller of New York State. Altogether, we pledged enough equity capital to enable Percy to go to Chemical Bank for a $2 million loan, which would give us the money to pay Harry Novick his asking price and give us some startup capital.

There was a hitch when Harry Novick discovered that I was one of the investors. He told Percy that employees of the station could not become owners and that I could not be part of the deal. Needless to say, Percy needed my $20,000. He also needed my expertise, so he was pretty upset when he called me. But I knew that Harry Novick was just trying to keep me out of the deal because of what had gone on between us. I assured Percy that I was an independent contractor, not an em-

Ruth Brown, Hal, and Roberta Flack, 1980s

ployee, and that although my paycheck came from WLIB, the money came from the sponsors.

Then I read through the purchase agreement and found a problem. There was nothing in the agreement about WLIB-FM, and, as the person responsible for most of the programming on WLIB-FM, I knew its potential as a moneymaker.

FM stations were beginning to dominate the broadcasting of recorded music by that time because of their superior reproduction of high fidelity and stereo signals. I told Percy, "We must have the option for the FM station. You are buying the AM station, but FM is where the future is. This agreement has to include an option to buy WLIB-FM."

I also told Percy that we should set the price for the FM station at that time. I suggested $1 million. I was certain that the value of the FM station was going to skyrocket and if we didn't set the price, we would not be able to afford to exercise the option in the future.

Novick was trying to take advantage of a tax break that was available to him for only a short time, and he was so anxious to close the deal that he agreed to the option I suggested.

The deal was approved by the Federal Communications Commission, and at a big contract signing, all of the investors in Inner City Broadcasting signed the document of sale. In 1971, Inner City Broadcasting took over WLIB-AM. It was a historic moment for a group of Black investors.

But our euphoria didn't last long. It turned out that Harry Novick had been working hard to undermine our investment before we had even made it. He had been building a new broadcast headquarters downtown and quietly transferring as much of the business of WLIB-AM to the FM station, which he had renamed WBLS. By the time we took over, he had persuaded most of the major sponsors to make the move to WBLS. He took most of the WLIB-AM personnel with him downtown, leaving us with a group of seven or eight White engineers, whose union contract provided that they get paid whether they worked or not. Needless to say, this did not help our cash flow problem. Add to all this the heavy competition from WWRL and WBLS, both 24-hour stations aimed at the same market as WLIB, and the future did not look auspicious.

I threw myself into the job of programming for the station, attracting more advertisers, cutting costs wherever possible, and getting the word out about the "new" WLIB. I brought in Ken Williams, who was born in Jamaica and had been doing a West Indian program on WNJR. He did a Caribbean music show on WLIB on Saturdays and Sundays and attracted cash advertisers from New York's West Indian community. This helped to increase our cash flow, because most of the regular sponsors had deferred billing agreements.

Doing much of the programming myself also helped to save money. I had Eddie O'Jay on in the morning, from sign-on until 10 A.M. Joe Bostic took over with a four-hour gospel show. Then, at 2 P.M., I came on and continued until sign-off, which could be anywhere from 6 P.M. to 9 P.M., depending on the season. David Lampel and Scott Gorman did the news. If cash flow was an especially big problem, I could forego my paycheck, but I tried hard to make sure we could get enough money over the weekend from the West Indian advertisers to cover the other employees' checks by Monday.

Eventually, however, we had to confront the issue of the engineers, who were the only ones allowed to work the tapes and records at WLIB. By agreement with the engineers union, none of the disc jockeys could even touch the equipment. They were separated from it by glass booths. The union contract prevented us from reducing the number of engineers, and being forced to use an all-White crew made it even more painful to scrape up the money to pay them week after week.

But the main issue was the bottom line. Pierre "Pepe" Sutton, Percy's son, was vice president of WLIB, and eventually he terminated all but three of the engineers—two to operate the transmitter and one to handle tape at the station. We brought the turntables into the disc jockeys' studio and had the announcers play the records themselves. Needless to say, the union wasn't about to take this lying down. The fight was long, bitter, and especially painful for me, a longtime union man.

That first year was very difficult, and it was obvious to most of us at Inner City Broadcasting that if we were going to make it we were going to have to exercise the option to buy WBLS. Considering the money problems we already had, this might have seemed foolish, but from a business standpoint it made sense to take over a competitor that was getting stronger. Fortunately, the price had been set in the original agreement, so we didn't have to haggle over that. But that $1 million might as well have been $10 million, as poor as we were.

The first step was to come up with the $150,000 down payment on the option. Mutual Broadcasting offered to cover both the option payment and the balance of the purchase price in exchange for stock in Inner City, but we wanted to keep the ownership of the company Black.

Fortunately, Clarence Jones was able to secure a personal loan against his stock in the company and come up with the option down payment. The deadline for raising the balance came and went, and we still didn't have it; and it took some very delicate negotiations to get Harry Novick to agree to extend the date for closing the deal. For the balance, we went back to Chemical Bank, which had loaned us the initial $2 million to buy WLIB.

I'll never forget that meeting at Chemical. Percy Sutton, chairman of the board, his son Pepe, who by this time was president of Inner City, Bill Tatum, Dorothy Brunson, and I represented Inner City, and we had to sit there and be reminded that we had not paid off a cent on the principal of the original loan. The only thing in our favor was that WBLS was a profitable station, as the figures we had brought along showed. We argued and they argued. We negotiated and they negotiated. After a marathon two-day session, we finally struck a deal.

We agreed to find individual cosigners for $300,000 of the loan, as a guarantee that certain monies would be paid by a deadline set by the bank, or else it could seize any property or funds used as a guarantee. Most of the cosigners for this $300,000 were original investors, who pledged property in amounts ranging from $25,000 to $50,000. They included Robert Seevy, an attorney and real estate man; John Edmonds, our lawyer; Harriet Pitt, a public relations adviser who was working very closely with us; as well as Carl McCall, Bill Tatum, Oliver and Percy Sutton, and myself.

Chemical Bank stipulated that an additional $300,000 of the loan had to come from Van Camp, a Boston-based MESBIC (Minority Enterprise Small Business Investment Company), whose whole operation centered around investing money from private sources in minority-owned businesses. There were representatives from Van Camp at that meeting, and there was little we could do but accept the bank's stipulation, even though this meant giving up on the idea of Inner City being entirely Black-owned. With all the strings attached to that particular loan, we ended up signing over about 40 percent of the equity in Inner City Broadcasting to Van Camp. Still, the deal had gone through, and Inner City Broadcasting proudly announced that it now owned two stations. Only those of us on the inside knew that ICBC only had about $100 in its checking account.

Both WLIB in Harlem and WBLS downtown were restructured under the umbrella of Inner City Broadcasting. I was named vice president of WBLS and moved to the station's headquarters at 43rd Street and Second Avenue. I was reluctant to give up my positions as programming manager and deejay of my own show at WLIB. After thirty years on the air, it was really strange not to have my own show. But I knew as well as (and in some cases, better than) my partners that WBLS was the profit-maker and that if we were to make our venture work, we had to make that station even more profitable. My experience in all phases of the radio business made me a critically important part of the team.

We brought in Frankie Crocker to manage programming at WBLS. He established an urban contemporary format—WBLS was a pioneer in that format—that would appeal to a crossover audience. Although he came up with the slogan, "WBLS, the Black experience in radio," he also aimed to appeal to Whites by featuring Black music currently on the pop charts. He did a great job recruiting a program staff of rather flamboyant announcers who played a mix of soul, jazz, and Latin. This on-air talent included Vy Higginson, Kenny Webb, Lamar Renee, and Al Roberts. Dick Novick, Harry's son, remained in charge of sales until we brought in Marvin Sellers from WWRL. WBLS really took off, and with its revenues as a cushion, Inner City Broadcasting was also able to build up WLIB.

With the urban contemporary format established on WBLS, we switched to a talk-and-news format on WLIB. The slogan was "Your Total News and Information Station." After we started attracting a bigger audience, a lot of other Black-oriented AM stations followed suit. Most importantly, we were able to start paying off those huge loans.

By 1975, I was feeling pretty good about what I was doing in radio and for young Black people, but I wanted to do more, so I decided to set up a scholarship fund at my alma mater, Howard University. I didn't have enough money to do it on my own; but I had a lot of friends. Some of them decided it was time to honor me, so they planned a big dinner at the Grand Ballroom of the New York Hilton. Tickets were $100 per person, with the proceeds going to the Hal Jackson Scholarship Foundation.

What a night that was. It was called "The House That Jack Built," and Isaac Hayes and Melba Moore cohosted the star-studded event. Dinner chairpersons were Ruth Bowen, president of the Queen Booking Agency (who had represented many celebrities, including Dinah Washington), Ahmet Ertegun, chairman of Atlantic Records, Roberta Flack, and Congressman Charles Rangel. Honorary chairpersons were Prime Minister Eric Gairy of Grenada, West Indies; Percy Sutton, my friend, business partner, and president of the Borough of Manhattan; Mayor Robert F. Wagner; and Mayor Walter E. Washington of Washington, D.C.

Celebrities from the worlds of entertainment, business, and politics packed the place. I was especially pleased to see Denise Dumaine, Miss Talented Teen International 1974, who had come all the way from Missouri with her chaperone for the event. Among those who made speeches were Ahmet Ertegun, Pepe Sutton, Ruth Bowen, Gloria Thomas, Billy Rowe, Gloria Toote, Frankie Crocker, and Congressman Charles Rangel.

Deputy Mayor Paul Gibson presented me with the key to the city; Bernard Jackson brought greetings from Governor Hugh Carey, and a proclamation was read from Percy Sutton as Manhattan borough president. Entertainment was provided by Melba Moore and Isaac Hayes as well as by the Ohio Players, the Manhattans, and Ralph Carter of the popular television program *Good Times*. A lot of money was raised that night for the Hal Jackson Scholarship Foundation, and I was especially pleased to be able to announce a special scholarship to Howard University's Department of Communications to help aspiring young people get started in the world of media that had been so much a part of my life.

By the following year, all my media experience was put to the test again when Frankie Crocker, whom we all regarded as key to the success of WBLS, was indicted on charges of perjury during a federal grand jury payola investigation. (That conviction was overturned on appeal two years later, and Frankie went to work as an artists and records consultant with Polydor Records in California. He would rejoin WBLS twice over the next twenty years.) It was panic time in the Inner City Broadcasting boardroom. Since I was the only one on the board with programming experience, I was asked to step in. I did, taking on the creative operation of WBLS in addition to my other duties.

For the next two years, I handled all the programming for the station, and I took the opportunity to move it more into the mainstream. I dropped the "Black Experience in Radio" tag and came up with a new slogan—"World's Best-Looking Sound"—and chose more danceable music. I also hired on more low-key announcers and added magazine-style news reports and tasteful commercials. I felt that it was time for WBLS to grow up and be more sophisticated, and I am pleased to say that my strategy worked. We grossed unbelievable advertising revenues, and the New York City–based Arbitron (one of the largest media-rating services) announced that WBLS edged out WABC as the number one station in the nation.

Black-owned stations had traditionally fared poorly in the ratings; this was a serious matter, since ad agencies used the ratings to scout stations for their clients. Back in 1973, WDAS in Philadelphia had sued Arbitron for $2.5 million in damages, claiming that Arbitron had caused them to lose ad revenue by rating them inaccurately. The suit was eventually dropped after Arbitron agreed to change its rating methods. Despite the agreement, rating services like Arbitron seemed reluctant to admit that Black people actually listen to radio. The fact that Arbitron rated us number one showed just how successful we had become.

AUTO WHOLESALERS

HAL JACKSON
TWO SHOWS DAILY!

| 6:00 TO 7:45 **A.M.** | 11:00 TO 11:55 **P.M.** |

WEAM • 1390
MUTUAL IN WASHINGTON

11.

REBUILDING JACK'S HOUSE

ot long after I took over the programming at WBLS, we consolidated Inner City Broadcasting downtown at Second Avenue and 43rd Street. Percy Sutton made a bid for the Democratic mayoral nomination in 1976, and when he was unsuccessful, he finished out his second term as Manhattan borough president and retired from public office. Once he came on with us full-time, we really expanded the scope of Inner City Broadcasting.

We wanted Inner City to be a nationwide media corporation, and to that end we wanted to acquire radio stations in other parts of the country. Unfortunately, Chemical Bank didn't share our vision. We couldn't put our finger on it, but we had the definite impression that race played a part in the bank's reluctance to back us in our proposed new ventures. It seemed that it was okay to invest in ICBC as long as we didn't get too ambitious, but we were not staying "in our place." We went to some other banks and eventually secured the financing necessary to expand the way we wanted to. We also used that financing to buy out Van Camp's interest in Inner City Broadcasting in 1977, ending up paying them about $700,000 on the original $300,000 loan.

The first station we added was in Detroit, and we named it WBLS. Not long after, we had the opportunity to acquire KRE-AM and FM in San Francisco. As vice chairman in charge of programming at ICBC, it was my job to take charge of these new stations, hire staff, and program them so they would have that certain "BLS feeling," which is hard to define but which basically reflected what I had done at WBLS after the departure of Frankie Crocker: low-key, sophisticated, wide-ranging in terms of the music played, appealing to a broad audience. We renamed the San Francisco station KBLX, and we built it into a major station, especially after we developed and built out the FM frequency—we installed a signal on Mount St. Bruno.

In order to build up these stations I had to spend a lot of time away from New York. After ICBC acquired two stations in Los Angeles, I actually relocated there for a time, although I still kept my apartment in New York. Alice and I had parted ways by then, although we remained friends, and there was really nothing keeping me in New York because I didn't have my own show.

KUTE, the Los Angeles FM station, was fairly easy to take over and continue as a general-market station. The AM station, originally called KGFJ but renamed KKTT by its most recent owners, was a much greater challenge. It was a very small neighborhood station with a 1,000-watt signal during the day and only a 280-watt signal at night. I really made building up that station my pet project. We changed the name back to KGFJ; and I held a big "Welcome Back KGFJ" party in MacArthur Park in downtown Los Angeles. Thousands of people turned out for the party and helped us get off to a good start. I had decided to make it a youth-oriented station, which was not difficult for me because of my lifelong involvement with young people. I have always liked to surround myself with young people and listen to what they have to say and take my cues from them about what's in and what's new.

Wherever I go, I get involved in the Black community, and I was deeply enmeshed in local LA affairs in no time—Christmas food and toy drives, antidrug programs, and lots of other community projects being supported and promoted by the stations. Trophies and plaques were beginning to pile up in my office on Riverside Drive in Los Angeles when I saw the opportunity to use the power of Inner City Broadcasting as a national force for good.

The 1980–1981 Atlanta child murders appalled and riveted the attention of the nation, but many of us felt the local authorities and the FBI were not doing enough to try to solve the mystery and stop the killings. In order to focus attention on the situation and show that people all over the country wanted the murders solved, I organized nighttime marches in New York, Los Angeles, and San Francisco. The marchers carried lighted candles. We had about 12,000 people on the New York march and as many as 40,000 in Los Angeles. Although publicity for ICBC's radio stations was not my paramount concern in organizing those marches, the fact that they were covered by network television and even the international media, and that this coverage included mention of ICBC, was very successful from a public relations standpoint.

By 1982, ICBC was twenty-first on the *Black Enterprise* magazine list of the top Black-owned businesses in the nation. We had 250 employees nationwide, assets of $65 million, and a $24 million gross for that year. Needless to say, the original investors had made their money back many times over.

We had made a few mistakes, mostly because some of our ideas were ahead of their time. We wanted to get into television, and in 1981 we bought the Apollo Theater at a bankruptcy sale. The four-story building, erected in 1913 by the Schiffman family, had become a symbol of Harlem in its heyday. It had a rich history of Black talent. Many greats had gotten their start there, among them Ella Fitzgerald, Dinah Washington, and Sammy Davis Jr. I had wonderful memories of emceeing shows at the Apollo and seeing all that great talent, but by the 1970s the Apollo wasn't what it used to be—for that matter, neither was Harlem—and in 1978, the Schiffman family closed the theater because they were losing too much money.

Under Percy Sutton's leadership, we had the idea of renovating the Apollo and putting in a state-of-the-art recording studio and television production facilities. We formed the Apollo Entertainment Network and planned to originate television programming from the theater 24 hours a day. We spent $20 million on the renovation. In 1985, the Apollo Theater reopened to celebrate its fiftieth anniversary, and the following July, we held the finals of the Hal Jackson's Talented Teens International contest at the Apollo for the first time. The 1991, 1992, 1995, 1996, and 1998 contests were also held at the Apollo. Although we produced *It's Showtime at the Apollo*, a nationally syndicated TV program, which is still aired on Saturday nights, the new Apollo did not, as we had hoped, become a world-class cultural magnet. In 1992, we had to cut our losses and transfer ownership to the Apollo Theater Foundation, a nonprofit group that might better be able to raise funds to keep it operating.

But we got into television in other ways, primarily by buying cable franchises, because we all recognized that cable was the future. We were granted part of the Queens, New York, franchise, and Percy was able to arrange franchises for ICBC in several cities, including Detroit, Philadelphia, and Washington, DC. Inner City Broadcasting fared much better.

Oliver Sutton died in 1983, and in 1990 Percy turned over the operations of lCBC to his son Pepe. But in spite of these changes, the company continues to grow and prosper. I am proud that I had the vision to be one of the original investors, and the skill and experience to bring to the programming of the various radio stations ICBC acquired.

By 1982, Inner City Broadcasting was doing very well, and as its vice president, so was I. (Later, I became the company's group chairman.) Not only was I comfortable financially, but I was in the business I had loved since I was a kid. I achieved some recognition for what I was doing with the Los Angeles AM station, KGFJ, when I received the award for Program Director of the Year from Black Radio Exclusive in 1982. I was spending most of my time in Los Angeles, although I traveled a lot.

As frequently as I could, I attended the local contests for the Hal Jackson's Talented Teens International pageant, helping whenever possible to raise the visibility of the pageant and keep it going. I often returned to New York to take care of ICBC business, and to visit my daughter Jewell, who had married Gene McCabe, president of North General Hospital.

Jewell has become one of the best-known women in the country. She came up with the idea of starting the National Coalition of 100 Black Women (NCBW) back in the mid-1970s, and I backed her financially, via an anonymous donation. She says it was my example and advice that inspired her to do it: "My father is a communicator. He invented himself at a time when there was no minority portfolio in America."

I would always tell my children, "If you don't see yourself (as a people) in major media, both print and electronic (on the front page of *The New York Times*, the *Chicago Tribune*, *The Washington Post*, the *Los Angeles Times*, or the *Atlanta Constitution*), politically you have no currency in America. You're not part of the marketplace. If you don't see yourself on the major television networks, if you don't hear yourself on the radio, you don't exist in the minds of the policymakers, the movers and shakers in America." Jewell took that advice to heart.

Her mother, at whose kitchen table the most influential Black women in the nation sat at one time or another, also inspired her over the years. In a mere ten months, Jewell managed to organize in twenty states and the District of Columbia, and by 1982 there were thirty-seven chapters of the NCBW. Its membership is dedicated to addressing the economic and social needs of Black women and preparing the next generation to enter the new millennium fueled by the sense of historic continuity and social responsibility that characterize the legacy of Black women and volunteerism in the United States. At this writing, the NCBW is approaching two decades of serving and developing a voice for Black women.

When I traveled to New York, I visited Alice's son, Gerald, who had remained with me after Alice and I split up. He had inherited a lot of his mother's talent. At the age of 16, he was writing and doing the arranging for an eighteen-piece band.

I also stopped in Washington, D.C., to check on my scholarship fund at Howard University, raise more money for it, and visit my older daughter, Jane Harley, and her three sons, Eugene, Edmond, and Eric. Jane had spent most of her career in D.C. classrooms and had designed the After-School Creative Arts program, which Amy Carter took an active part in at the Stevens School. After all the publicity that program received because of the involvement of the president's daughter, Jane moved into a supervisory position in the schools.

My son, Hal Junior, whom we all called Jacky, lives in Milwaukee. At the age of 30 he became the youngest state Supreme Court judge in the country. He had attended Colgate University and been a football star, but after an injury he quit college. My former mother-in-law wanted him to go to work, but I had insisted he finish his education and got him into Marquette University in Wisconsin, where he finished law school.

Putting all three children through college wasn't easy. There was a twelve-year period of my life when I didn't take a single day's vacation because of all those college bills I had to pay.

There was just one area of my life that wasn't perfect: I didn't have a woman to share it with, although I had lady friends and didn't lack for companionship—Debi and I were close, but we hadn't married yet. Well, actually there was one other area: I had not had my own radio show in more than a decade, and I missed being on the air.

I was 67 years old—retirement age for most people. I had worked hard all of my life and had every right to sit back and rest on my laurels—or at least to slow down a bit. But I had always been a workaholic; if I stopped working, I had no idea what I would do. Working was like breathing to me. So when the opportunity arose for me to go back on the air with a music show, I jumped at the chance.

For a long time, I had worried that the classics were missing from the airwaves. By classics, I mean the great songs from all categories by all the great singers. There was no radio show where you could hear Bobby Blue Bland along with Barbra Streisand, B. B. King along with Peggy Lee, Count Basie along with Sade. There were a number of White artists who were really getting into the blues and gospel and jazz, but you couldn't find them on radio stations aimed at the Black market. I had been thinking about this a lot when a slot on Sunday mornings opened up at WBLS. When we had a meeting to discuss how to fill it, I found myself suggesting that I go back on the air. That was how *Sunday Morning Classics* was born.

I moved my main base of operations back to New York, giving up the day-to-day administrative duties in the programming end of ICBC and taking the position of group chairman, which had fewer day-to-day responsibilities. I concentrated on making the show—which was taped and then aired from 8 to 10 A.M. Sundays—a hit.

I played the kind of music I wanted. I had no philosophy, I just chose the records according to gut feelings. I played what I considered great songs, no matter what race the artists were. I played records by New Kids on the Block, who recorded for Berry Gordy's Motown Records. Those kids were good, and when they came down from Massachusetts to audition for me, I called up the Apollo Theater that very night and helped get them on that stage. Maurice Starr, a Black man, was their manager, and even though the color of their skin was not Black, I felt the depth of their feeling for their music.

I also played cuts from George Michael's crossover album, *Faith*, even though I knew I was going to be criticized for playing him when many Black artists where not getting the kind of exposure he got in the pop arena. It was not only White artists who didn't get their shot on Black radio. Tracy Chapman was not played on a lot of Black stations, and I certainly played her records.

It all comes down to survival. If you want to get mass numbers, you naturally have to try to open up your format. I have always been concerned with showcasing Black artists, but I don't think you can eliminate other performers.

Now, I didn't just push buttons. Anyone can do that. As in the old days on *The House That Jack Built*, I talked to my listeners and tried to establish a comfortable atmosphere. Not long after the show was up and running, I switched from tape to live format. I talked about the performers and gave background information on the songs. I had been around so long that I had personal anecdotes about everyone from Dinah Washington to Tina Turner to Billie Holiday to the Jackson Five. I started doing live on-air interviews with singers like Roberta Flack, Stevie Wonder, and Nancy Wilson. Fortunately, the trend was swinging back to personality radio, and I took advantage of it.

Pretty soon, my ratings were so good that the show was extended from two hours to four hours. I could not have been happier except when, a couple of years later, it was extended again, to six hours, from 8 A.M. to 2 P.M., and a couple of years after that, to eight hours, from 8 am to 4 P.M. It continued to draw the highest ratings in the Sunday morning time slot; in fact, our ratings were higher than the next six of our competitors combined. By that time, the show was heard not just in the New York area but also as far away as the Caribbean. In August 1993, American Urban Radio Networks began offering prerecorded segments to some of its 225 affiliates nationwide.

Even more happiness came into my life when I married Debi, who, using the on-air name Debi B, became one of my two cohosts. The other was Clay Berry, who also served as engineer.

In 1989 I celebrated my fiftieth year in the radio business. This was a big year for me. On November 2, the Apollo Theater stage came alive again with tributes and performances by the Reverend Jesse Jackson, Arthur Prysock, Bobby Brown, Eartha Kitt, Ronnie Spector, Ahmet Ertegun, Coretta Scott King, Berry Gordy, and Percy Sutton. Those who could not be there in person sent tapes; among them were Michael Jackson, Eddie Murphy, Stevie Wonder, and Lionel Ritchie.

That same year, the U.S. House of Representatives honored me for fifty years in broadcasting. The following year, I was given the Broadcasting Hall of Fame Award by the National Association of Broadcasters at the annual convention in Atlanta. CBS News correspondent Charles Osgood was inducted at the same time. And in 1991, I received the William Bethany Award and the Candace Award from the National Coalition of 100 Black Women. (There may have been a little nepotism in that latter award, since my daughter, Jewell Jackson McCabe, is president of the NCBW.) The following year, I was honored with a Radio Living Legend award.

Then, in 1995, I received what I feel is the greatest honor of my career. In October, the Museum of Broadcast Communications inducted me into the Radio Hall of Fame. The same year, the museum recognized two other African Americans along with me; the three of us became the first Blacks ever to receive the honor. After I had made my speech and returned to my table, the first thing I said to Debi was, "I finally made it."

Other honors and awards followed, including formal recognition by the Smithsonian Institution for my collaborative efforts in the making of the Smithsonian Productions' award-winning radio series, *Black Radio: Telling It Like It Was* in October 1997. In April 1998, the Rock and Roll Hall of Fame in Cleveland honored me for my contribution to the field of broadcast. And in February 2000, New York Governor George Pataki held a reception in my honor at the Schomberg Institute, where I received a Distinguished Service Award.

I am pleased to report that I recently passed another milestone in my life; I celebrated my sixtieth anniversary in broadcasting. The National Association of Black-Owned Broadcasters honored me with a Lifetime Achievement Award. And in November 1999, a star-studded tribute was held in my honor in the Rainbow Room at New York's Rockefeller Center. I was blessed to have a bevy of loved ones, friends, and supporters take part in that tribute. President Clinton filmed a short video tribute, which was shown to the audience. He also sent a letter of personal congratulations in which he wrote, "You have been a leader and pioneer in Black radio, and you can be proud of your contributions to the industry and to the African-American community through six decades of dynamic challenge and change."

Those are humbling, inspiring, and gratifying words, and all I can do is keep striving to deserve that kind of praise from the people whom I most admire.

While I appreciate the honors, what I appreciate most is the opportunities I have had to serve my community and my nation through the medium of radio. It wasn't easy for me to break into the field, but once I did, I really found a home. I'm proud to say that the *Sunday Morning Classics* is still one of the most popular shows on New York City radio.

I've watched the medium grow and have had the great good fortune to grow with it. Even though I've had my fair share of setbacks in life, I've always believed I could accomplish whatever I set out to do, and to a large extent I've been successful. Many, many years ago, I heard a poem that expressed my philosophy of life so exactly that I learned it by heart. It has helped me a lot through the years.

If you think you are beaten, you are;
If you think you dare not, you don't.
If you'd like to win, but think you can't,
It's almost a cinch you won't.

If you think you'll lose, you're lost,
For out of the world we find
Success begins with a person's will;
It's all in the state of mind.

Life's battles don't always go
To the stronger or faster man;
But sooner or later the man who wins
Is the one who thinks he can.